Company's Coming

PASTA

To Bev
Jazz it up !
Jean Paré

by
Jean Paré

Cover Photo

PASTA

First Edition April, 1990

I.S.B.N. 0-9693322-2-X

Published and Distributed by
Company's Coming Publishing Limited
Box 8037, Station "F"
Edmonton, Alberta, Canada
T6H 4N9

Printed in Canada

Cookbooks in the Company's Coming series by Jean Paré:

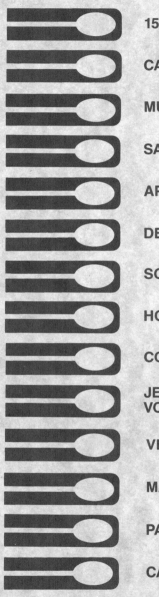

table of Contents

the Jean Paré story

Jean Paré was born and raised during the Great Depression in Irma, a small farm town in eastern Alberta. She grew up understanding that the combination of family, friends and home cooking is the essence of a good life. Jean learned from her mother, Ruby Elford, to appreciate good cooking and was encouraged by her father, Edward Elford, who praised even her earliest attempts. When she left home she took with her many acquired family recipes, her love of cooking and her intriguing desire to read recipe books like novels!

While raising a family of four, Jean was always busy in her kitchen preparing delicious, tasty treats and savory meals for family and friends of all ages. Her reputation flourished as the mom who would happily feed the neighborhood.

In 1963, when her children had all reached school age, Jean volunteered to cater to the 50th anniversary of the Vermilion School of Agriculture, now Lakeland College. Working out of her home, Jean prepared a dinner for over 1000 people which launched a flourishing catering operation that continued for over eighteen years. During that time she was provided with countless opportunities to test new ideas with immediate feedback — resulting in empty plates and contented customers! Whether preparing cocktail sandwiches for a house party or serving a hot meal for 1500 people, Jean Paré earned a reputation for good food, courteous service and reasonable prices.

"Why don't you write a cookbook?" Time and again Jean was asked that question as requests for her recipes mounted. Jean's response was to team up with her son Grant Lovig in the fall of 1980 to form Company's Coming Publishing Limited. April 14, 1981 marked the debut of "150 DELICIOUS SQUARES", the first Company's Coming cookbook in what soon would become Canada's most popular cookbook series. Jean released a new title each year for the first six years. The pace quickened and by 1987 the company had begun publishing two titles each year.

Jean Paré's operation has grown from the early days of working out of a spare bedroom in her home to operating a large and fully equipped test kitchen in Vermilion, near the home she and her husband Larry built. Full time staff has grown steadily to include marketing personnel located in major cities across Canada. Home office is located in Edmonton, Alberta where distribution, accounting and administration functions are headquartered. Company's Coming cookbooks are now distributed throughout Canada and the United States plus numerous overseas markets.

Jean Paré's approach to cooking has always called for easy to follow recipes using mostly common, affordable ingredients. Her wonderful collection of time-honored recipes, many of which are family heirlooms, are a welcome addition to any kitchen. That's why we say: taste the tradition.

Foreword

Of all the foods known to us, pasta rates as one of the most versatile. Not only is it adaptable to just about any vegetable, meat or fish one might have on hand, but it is also quick and easy to prepare. The array of plain and fancy dry pasta available is economical and stores well. In this cookbook you will find many ways of preparing hot and cold pasta dishes, even a few desserts!

Plenty of water is needed when cooking to allow free movement of pasta. The addition of cooking oil will help prevent it from boiling over or clumping together. Stir occasionally. Cooking al dente (ahl-DEN-tay), which means tender but firm, is most desirable. The surest way to know when pasta is properly cooked is to repeatedly sample it as cooking progresses. Bite a piece to ensure that it is tender but still offers some resistance to the tooth.

Times given in this cookbook are for commercially available dry pasta. The homemade variety of fresh pasta cooks in as little as half the time, depending upon thickness and tends to absorb liquid more quickly. Watch carefully as it can become soft, sticky and mushy. Remember, pasta doubles in size when cooked. A colander is best for draining pasta.

Olive oil and fresh Parmesan cheese are recommended ingredients but any cooking oil and packaged grated Parmesan cheese may be substituted. Freshly ground pepper is a welcome finishing touch to any pasta dish especially salads. A kitchen scale is handy too, as recipes usually call for pasta by weight. If interchanging different sizes and kinds of pasta in a recipe be sure to use the correct weight indicated.

Could anyone think of pasta without thinking of Italy? Today, nearly every nationality delights in pasta. For an international flavor, try Italian Carbonara from Italy, Pastitsio from Greece and Pot Stickers from China, to name a few.

Pasta is at its best when cooked and served immediately but can easily be frozen. Casseroles, sauces and the many varieties of shaped and fancy pasta are equally adaptable to freezing. Stock your cupboard with pasta. Whether planning ahead or deciding on the spur of the moment, choose pasta when company's coming.

Jean Paré

STUFFED SHELLS

Terrific hot dinner appetizers. Stuffed with a meat-spinach filling and cooked with a tomato sauce topping. Cook extra shells to allow for tearing.

Jumbo pasta shells	40	40
Boiling water	4 qts.	5 L
Cooking oil (optional)	1 tbsp.	15 mL
Salt	1 tbsp.	15 mL
Ground beef	¾ lb.	375 g
Finely chopped onion	⅓ cup	75 mL
Cooking oil	1 tbsp.	15 mL
Frozen chopped spinach, thawed, cooked and squeezed to drain	10 oz.	284 g
Dry bread crumbs	⅓ cup	75 mL
Grated Parmesan cheese	⅓ cup	75 mL
Salt	1 tsp.	5 mL
Pepper	¼ tsp.	1 mL
Garlic powder	¼ tsp.	1 mL
Eggs, beaten	3	3
Tomato sauce, see page 38	1 cup	250 mL
Grated Parmesan cheese (or use 3 times as much grated mozzarella cheese)	½ cup	125 mL

Cook shells in boiling water, first amounts of cooking oil and salt in uncovered Dutch oven until just barely tender but firm, about 12 to 15 minutes. Stir occasionally. Drain. Rinse with cold water. Drain well.

Scramble-fry ground beef and onion in remaining cooking oil until browned.

Add next 7 ingredients to beef in pan. Mix. Remove from heat. Stuff shells using 2 rounded teaspoonfuls each. Put into greased 9 x 9 inch (22 x 22 cm) pan.

Pour tomato sauce over shells, being sure to get some on each one. Sprinkle with Parmesan cheese. Cover. Bake in 350ºF (180ºC) oven for about 35 to 40 minutes until hot and cheese is melted. For a dinner appetizer, serve 2 per person. Allow more if serving as main course. Freeze leftover filling. Makes 40 stuffed jumbo shells.

Pictured without sauce on page 143.

SPINACH STUFFED SHELLS

Contains cottage cheese. Cooked in a zesty meat sauce.

MEAT SAUCE

Ground beef	½ lb.	250 g
Chopped onion	2 tbsp.	30 mL
Cooking oil	2 tsp.	10 mL
Tomato paste	5½ oz.	156 mL
Water	1¼ cups	300 mL
Salt	1 tsp.	5 mL
Parsley flakes	¼ tsp.	1 mL
Oregano	⅛ tsp.	0.5 mL
Garlic powder	⅛ tsp.	0.5 mL
Basil	⅛ tsp.	0.5 mL
Jumbo pasta shells	20	20
Boiling water	2½ qts.	3 L
Cooking oil (optional)	1 tbsp.	15 mL
Salt	2 tsp.	10 mL

FILLING

Frozen chopped spinach, thawed and squeezed to drain	10 oz.	284 g
Cottage cheese	1 cup	250 mL
Grated mozzarella cheese	1 cup	250 mL
Grated Parmesan cheese	2 tbsp.	30 mL

Meat Sauce: Scramble-fry meat and onion in first amount of cooking oil until no pink remains.

Add next 7 ingredients. Mix. Remove from heat.

Cook shells in boiling water, second amounts of cooking oil and salt in uncovered Dutch oven until tender but firm, about 12 to 15 minutes. Drain. Rinse with cold water. Drain well.

Filling: Mix all 4 ingredients together. Stuff shells using 2 rounded spoonfuls each.

Put ½ meat sauce in 9 × 9 inch (22 × 22 cm) pan. Lay shells on top. Spoon second ½ sauce over. Cover. Bake in 350°F (180°C) oven for about 30 to 40 minutes until bubbly hot. Makes 20 stuffed shells.

Pictured without sauce on page 143.

NUTTY CHEESE SHELLS

One bite appetizers. When served as a dinner appetizer in pink sauce it is quite dramatic. Sauce doubles for a dessert.

Large pasta shells (not jumbo)	24	24
Boiling water	2 qts.	2.5 L
Cooking oil (optional)	1 tbsp.	15 mL
Salt	2 tsp.	10 mL
Dofino cheese pieces, cut to fit	24	24
Chopped pecans or walnuts	¼ cup	60 mL

Cook shells in boiling water, cooking oil and salt in large uncovered saucepan until tender but firm, about 13 to 16 minutes. Stir occasionally. Drain. Rinse with cold water. Drain well.

Place cheese in shells. Put 3 to 5 pieces of nuts on top of each. Place in greased pan. Cover. Heat in 375°F (190°C) oven until hot and cheese is soft, about 1 to 2 minutes. Watch closely. Don't let it melt down too much. It should be soft enough to lose shape, not runny. Makes 24 stuffed shells.

DINNER APPETIZER

Cranberry juice	1 cup	250 mL
Granulated sugar	¼ cup	60 mL
Cornstarch	1 tbsp.	15 mL
Large or jumbo shells, stuffed and prepared as above		

Mix cranberry juice, sugar and cornstarch together in small saucepan over medium heat. Stir until it boils and thickens. Pour sauce onto small plates. Set 6 large shells in sauce. Serves 4.

Pictured on cover.

DESSERT SHELLS: Fill large (not jumbo) shells with your favorite chocolate or vanilla milk pudding. Piping makes it so easy. Set several shells in sauce used for Dinner Appetizer.

Paré Pointer

To make doughnuts, you must use hole milk.

An impressive appetizer. Contentment with every bite.

Jumbo pasta shells	40	40
Boiling water	4 qts.	5 L
Cooking oil (optional)	1 tbsp.	15 mL
Salt	1 tbsp.	15 mL
Chopped onion	1 cup	250 mL
Butter or margarine	½ cup	125 mL
Medium potatoes	6	6
Boiling salted water		
Half onion-butter mixture		
Grated medium Cheddar cheese	1½ cups	375 mL
Salt	1 tsp.	5 mL
Pepper	¼ tsp.	1 mL
Half onion-butter mixture		
Grated medium Cheddar cheese	½ cup	125 mL

Fresh chopped chives for garnish
   (optional)

Cook shells in first amount of boiling water, cooking oil and first amount of salt in uncovered Dutch oven until tender but firm, about 12 to 15 minutes. Stir occasionally. Drain. Rinse in cold water. Drain well.

Sauté onion in butter in saucepan until soft and clear. Set aside.

Cook potatoes in second amount of boiling water until tender. Drain. Mash.

Add ½ onion-butter mixture, first amount of cheese, second amount of salt and pepper to potato. Beat smooth. Stuff shells. Arrange in baking pan in single layer.

Put remaining ½ onion-butter mixture over top of stuffing followed by remaining cheese. If filling is hot, bake uncovered in 350°F (180°C) oven for about 10 minutes to melt cheese and brown a bit. If filling is cold, bake covered for 10 minutes and then uncovered for 10 minutes more.

Garnish with chives if desired. Makes 40 stuffed shells.

Pictured on page 143.

SALMON STUFFED SHELLS

Perfect large appetizers to serve hot.

Jumbo pasta shells	12	12
Boiling water	2 qts.	2.5 L
Cooking oil (optional)	1 tbsp.	15 mL
Salt	2 tsp.	10 mL
Egg	1	1
Cottage cheese	1 cup	250 mL
Dry onion flakes	1 tbsp.	15 mL
Parsley flakes	1 tsp.	5 mL
Salt	¼ tsp.	1 mL
Salmon, drained, skin and round bones removed, flaked (red looks best)	7¾ oz.	220 g
Lemon juice	1 tsp.	5 mL
Butter or margarine, melted	1 tbsp.	15 mL
Dry bread crumbs	¼ cup	60 mL
Grated Parmesan cheese	¼ cup	60 mL

Cook shells in boiling water, cooking oil and first amount of salt in large uncovered saucepan until tender but firm, about 12 to 15 minutes. Drain. Rinse with cold water. Drain well.

Beat egg, cottage cheese, onion, parsley and second amount of salt together. Stir in salmon and lemon juice. Stuff shells. Place round side down in 8 x 8 inch (20 x 20 cm) pan. Put 2 tbsp. (30 mL) water in bottom of pan.

Stir butter, crumbs and Parmesan cheese together. Sprinkle over top. Cover. Bake in 350ºF (180ºC) oven for about 30 minutes. Makes 12 shells. Serve 2 each for a dinner appetizer.

Pictured without crumb topping on page 143.

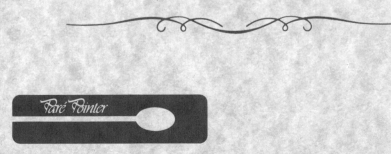

Paré Pointer

With a tire and some musicians you could have a rubber band.

SHRIMP NIBBLIES

These little morsels disappear quickly.

Large pasta shells (not jumbo)	48	48
Boiling water	2½ qts.	3 L
Cooking oil (optional)	1 tbsp.	15 mL
Salt	2 tsp.	10 mL
Grated medium Cheddar cheese	½ cup	125 mL
Salad dressing (such as Miracle Whip)	½ cup	125 mL
Broken shrimp, drained	4 oz.	113 g
Worcestershire sauce	1 tsp.	5 mL
Seasoned salt	⅛ tsp.	0.5 mL

Chopped parsley pieces, for garnish

Cook shells in boiling water, cooking oil and salt in uncovered Dutch oven until tender but firm, about 13 to 16 minutes. Stir occasionally. Drain. Rinse with cold water. Drain well.

Combine next 5 ingredients in blender. Blend smooth. Pipe into shells.

Top each shell with a bit of parsley if desired. Makes 48.

Pictured on page 143.

SHRIMP IN SHELLS: Put a dab of seafood sauce in each shell followed by a small canned or fresh, cooked shrimp.

BROTHY PASTA SOUP

No work to this. Simple and tasty.

Condensed beef consommé	10 oz.	284 mL
Water	1 cup	250 mL
Ditali or other small pasta	1 cup	250 mL
Canned vegetable juice (such as V8)	2 cups	500 mL

Grated Parmesan cheese, sprinkle

Combine consommé, water, raw pasta and juice in saucepan. Stir. Bring to a boil. Simmer covered for 10 minutes or until pasta is tender.

Serve with Parmesan cheese over top or passed at the table. Makes about 3½ cups (850 mL).

SHELLED ZUCCHINI SOUP

This colorful soup has a great flavor.

Mild Italian sausage, sliced ¼ inch (6 mm) thick	**8 oz.**	**250 g**
Chopped onion	**1 cup**	**250 mL**
Condensed chicken consommé	**2 × 10 oz.**	**2 × 284 mL**
Water	**3 cups**	**750 mL**
Garlic clove, minced	**1 - 2**	**1 - 2**
Coarsely grated zucchini, unpeeled	**4 cups**	**1 L**
Grated carrot	**1 cup**	**250 mL**
Italian seasoning	**1 tsp.**	**5 mL**
Basil	**½ tsp.**	**2 mL**
Oregano	**½ tsp.**	**2 mL**
Granulated sugar	**½ tsp.**	**2 mL**
Tiny pasta shells	**1 cup**	**250 mL**

Mozzarella cheese (optional)

Sauté sausage and onion in a large saucepan or Dutch oven until no pink remains in meat.

Add next 9 ingredients. Stir. Bring to a boil. Cover. Simmer slowly for at least 30 minutes or better yet, for 1 hour.

Add raw shells. Continue to simmer until shells are tender. Add more water if too thick.

This may be served now but if you'd like to dress it up, pour soup into broiler proof bowls, cover with mozzarella cheese and brown under broiler. Use up to 1 slice of cheese per bowl or use grated. Makes 8 cups (2 L).

Paré Pointer

We can't stop change. It is inevitable. Except from a vending machine, that is.

Beef stock can be interchanged for the bouillon. This is a real meal. Gratifying and full-bodied. A large recipe. Freeze leftovers.

Bacon slices, chopped	4	4
Chopped onion	1½ cups	375 mL
Lean ground beef	1½ lbs.	750 g
Beef bouillon cubes	10 × ⅕ oz.	10 × 6 g
Boiling water	10 cups	2.5 L
Canned tomatoes, broken up	14 oz.	398 mL
Chopped celery	1 cup	250 mL
Diced carrot	1 cup	250 mL
Diced potato	1½ cups	375 mL
Chopped cabbage, packed	1 cup	250 mL
Salt	1 tsp.	5 mL
Pepper	¼ tsp.	1 mL
Garlic powder	¼ tsp.	1 mL
Basil	½ tsp.	2 mL
Oregano	½ tsp.	2 mL
Fusilli (FOOZ-ee-lee)	8 oz.	250 g
Kidney beans or garbanzo, drained	14 oz.	398 mL

Scramble-fry bacon, onion and ground beef in Dutch oven to brown.

Dissolve bouillon cubes in boiling water. Add.

Add next 10 ingredients. Bring to a boil. Cover and simmer until vegetables are tender, about 25 minutes.

Add raw pasta and beans. Boil slowly for 10 minutes or until pasta is tender. Makes about 14 cups (3.5 L).

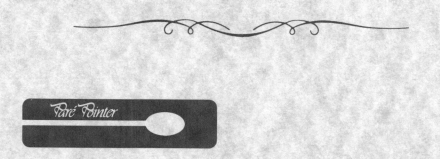

Paré Pointer

Not knowing what he might fall against on his way off the ladder, he fell against his will.

FAGIOLI SOUP

Fawj-OH-lee soup has a good flavor. Lots of beans and pasta. Broth is fairly thin.

Dried navy beans (dried white)	1 cup	250 mL
Water	8 cups	2 L
Ketchup	1 tbsp.	15 mL
Salt	1 tbsp.	15 mL
Pepper	¼ tsp.	1 mL
Garlic powder	½ tsp.	2 mL
Oregano	¼ tsp.	1 mL
Basil	¼ tsp.	1 mL
Bay leaf	1	1
Tiny pasta shells	1 cup	250 mL

Combine first 9 ingredients in large saucepan. Bring to a boil. Cover. Simmer slowly for about 1½ to 2 hours until beans are tender. Discard bay leaf.

Add raw shells. Simmer until tender, about 10 minutes. Stir occasionally. If too thick, add water. Makes about 6½ cups (1.7 L).

1. Rigatoni Broccoli Bake page 55
2. Fruit Pasta Salad page 21
3. Verm A Puff page 42
4. Shrimp Pasta Roll page 102
5. Corned Beef Roll page 103
6. Spinach Pasta Roll page 111

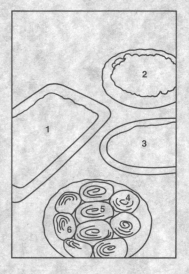

MACARONI BROCCOLI SOUP

With tomato juice as a base and broccoli for color contrast, this works out to be a good flavored soup.

Bacon slices, chopped	2	2
Tomato juice	3 cups	750 mL
Water	5 cups	1.25 L
Elbow macaroni	2 cups	500 mL
Broccoli flowerettes	1½ cups	375 mL
Salt	1 tsp.	5 mL
Pepper	¼ tsp.	1 mL
Garlic powder	¼ tsp.	1 mL
Basil	¼ tsp.	1 mL
Grated Parmesan cheese, sprinkle		

Brown bacon in Dutch oven over medium heat.

Add next 8 ingredients. Bring to a boil. Cover and simmer, stirring occasionally, until macaroni is tender, about 10 minutes.

Serve with a sprinkle of Parmesan cheese on top. Makes about 7 cups (1.75 L).

CHICKEN NOODLE SOUP

If you are lucky enough to have chicken stock on hand, use it instead of the bouillon cubes. A different soup and a good one.

Chicken bouillon cubes	8 x ⅕ oz.	8 x 6 g
Boiling water	8 cups	2 L
Cooked chicken or turkey, chopped	2 cups	500 mL
Frozen Chinese pea pods (or use fresh)	7 oz.	198 g
Soy sauce	2 tsp.	10 mL
Ginger	¼ tsp.	1 mL
Stars, alphabets and tubettini or fine egg noodles	6 oz.	170 g

Dissolve bouillon cubes in boiling water in large saucepan.

Add remaining ingredients. Bring to a boil. Cover. Boil gently until noodles are cooked, about 5 minutes. Makes about 8 cups (2 L).

Pictured on page 125.

MACARONI SHRIMP SALAD

Great combination. Great flavor. Great looks.

Elbow macaroni (or tiny shells)	2 cups	500 mL
Boiling water	2½ qts.	3 L
Cooking oil (optional)	1 tbsp.	15 mL
Salt	2 tsp.	10 mL
Salad dressing (such as Miracle Whip)	¾ cup	175 mL
Onion salt	¼ tsp.	1 mL
Pepper, sprinkle		
Small or broken shrimp, drained	4 oz.	113 g
Thinly sliced celery	1 cup	250 mL

Cook macaroni in boiling water, cooking oil and salt in uncovered Dutch oven until tender but firm, about 5 to 7 minutes. Drain. Rinse with cold water. Drain well. Return macaroni to pot.

Add salad dressing, onion salt and pepper. Toss well. Add shrimp and celery. Toss. Transfer to bowl to serve. Makes about 4½ cups (1.2 L).

VEGETABLE PASTA SALAD

Brightened with red and green strips of pepper and zucchini, this has a lively taste as well.

Rotini pasta	8 oz.	250 g
Boiling water	2½ qts.	3 L
Cooking oil (optional)	1 tbsp.	15 mL
Salt	2 tsp.	10 mL
Red pepper, slivered	1	1
Zucchini, unpeeled, slivered	2 cups	500 mL
Sliced green onions	¼ cup	60 mL
Fresh mushrooms, sliced	6	6
Sliced celery	½ cup	125 mL
Cooking oil	⅓ cup	75 mL
Red wine vinegar	¼ cup	60 mL
Grated Parmesan cheese	2 tbsp.	30 mL
Salt	1 tsp.	5 mL
Pepper	¼ tsp.	1 mL
Oregano	¼ tsp.	1 mL
Basil	¼ tsp.	1 mL
Garlic powder	¼ tsp.	1 mL

(continued on next page)

In large uncovered saucepan cook pasta in boiling water, cooking oil and first amount of salt until tender but firm. Drain. Rinse with cold water. Drain well. Return to pot.

Add next 5 ingredients to rotini in pot.

Mix remaining ingredients together in small bowl. Add to pot and toss well. Makes about 8 cups (2 L).

FRUIT PASTA SALAD

A pretty salad. Serve over shredded lettuce or in a lettuce cup. Garnish with cherries or strawberries.

Cappeletti, ditali or other pasta	8 oz.	250 g
Boiling water	2½ qts.	3 L
Cooking oil (optional)	1 tbsp.	15 mL
Salt	2 tsp.	10 mL
Pineapple tidbits, drained	14 oz.	398 mL
Fresh oranges, peeled and cut up	1 - 2	1 - 2
Seedless green and red grapes	1½ cups	375 mL
Fresh peach, peeled and cut up (if available)	1	1
Banana, sliced	1 - 2	1 - 2
DRESSING		
Plain yogurt	¾ cup	175 mL
Mayonnaise	⅓ cup	75 mL
Icing (confectioner's) sugar	¼ cup	60 mL
Finely grated lemon rind	½ tsp.	2 mL
Salt (scant)	⅛ tsp.	0.5 mL

Cook pasta in boiling water, cooking oil and salt in uncovered Dutch oven until tender but firm, about 6 to 8 minutes. Drain. Rinse with cold water. Drain well. Return pasta to pot.

Add pineapple, oranges and grapes.

Add banana just before adding dressing.

Dressing: Mix all ingredients together. Pour over salad. Toss. Serve in bowl. Makes about 6½ cups (1.5 L) salad.

Pictured on page 17.

TERIYAKI CHICKEN SALAD

Noodles centered with scrumptious chicken, feta cheese and trimmings.
Easy to double. Add a dinner roll and you have a picture perfect lunch.

Soy sauce	¼ cup	60 mL
Granulated sugar	1 tsp.	5 mL
Prepared mustard	½ tsp.	2 mL
Ginger	¼ tsp.	1 mL
Garlic powder	⅛ tsp.	0.5 mL
Boneless chicken breasts	2	2
Rotini	8 oz.	250 g
Boiling water	2½ qts.	3 L
Cooking oil (optional)	1 tbsp.	15 mL
Salt	2 tsp.	10 mL
DRESSING		
Vinegar	2 tbsp.	30 mL
Cooking oil	¼ cup	60 mL
Sugar	3 tbsp.	50 mL
Garlic salt	¼ tsp.	1 mL
Salt	¼ tsp.	1 mL
Pepper	⅛ tsp.	0.5 mL
Romaine lettuce or spinach leaves		
Crumbled feta cheese	½ cup	125 mL
Sliced pitted black olives	⅓ cup	75 mL
Chopped pimiento	2 - 4 tbsp.	30 - 60 mL

Stir first 5 ingredients together in bowl.

Add chicken. Turn to coat. Marinate for 20 minutes. Remove chicken and lay it on foil lined baking tray. Bake uncovered in 350°F (180°C) oven for about 30 minutes until tender. Brush with marinade every 10 minutes, turning once. Cool. Cut into small bite size pieces.

Cook pasta in boiling water, cooking oil and salt in uncovered Dutch oven until tender but firm, about 10 to 12 minutes. Drain. Rinse with cold water. Drain well. Return pasta to pot.

Dressing: Combine vinegar, cooking oil, sugar, salt, pepper and garlic powder together in small container. Stir well to dissolve sugar. Pour over pasta. Toss to coat.

Arrange lettuce leaves around outer edge of plates. Divide pasta among them.

(continued on next page)

Arrange chicken in center. Sprinkle olives over top. Sprinkle feta cheese around chicken. Surround chicken, olives and cheese with pimiento. Serves 2 for full meal or 4 as side salads.

Pictured on page 89.

TRAIL MIX SALAD

Very different and very good. Nutty and chewy.

Medium egg noodles	8 oz.	250 g
Boiling water	2½ qts.	3 L
Cooking oil (optional)	1 tbsp.	15 mL
Salt	2 tsp.	10 mL
Vinegar	2 tbsp.	30 mL
Cooking oil	1 - 2 tbsp.	15 - 30 mL
Granulated sugar	1 tbsp.	15 mL
Grated carrot	½ cup	125 mL
Shelled sunflower seeds	¼ cup	60 mL
Peanuts	¼ cup	60 mL
Broken cashews (or use chopped walnuts)	¼ cup	60 mL
Raisins	¼ cup	60 mL
Currants	¼ cup	60 mL
Salt	¼ tsp.	1 mL

Cook noodles in boiling water, first amounts of cooking oil and salt in uncovered Dutch oven until tender but firm, about 5 to 7 minutes. Drain. Rinse with cold water. Drain well. Return noodles to pot.

Stir vinegar, second amount of cooking oil and sugar together to dissolve sugar. Pour over pasta. Toss.

Add remaining ingredients. Toss well. Put into serving bowl. Makes about 5½ cups (1.25 L).

Pictured on page 107.

LAYERED PASTA SALAD

This is stunning when made in a large glass salad bowl. A good make ahead although it can be eaten sooner if needed.

Elbow macaroni	1½ cups	375 mL
Boiling water	2½ qts.	3 L
Cooking oil (optional)	1 tbsp.	15 mL
Salt	2 tsp.	10 mL
Olive oil (or cooking oil)	1 tbsp.	15 mL
Medium head of lettuce	1	1
Slivered cooked ham	1 cup	250 mL
Hard-boiled eggs, sliced	6	6
Frozen peas, cooked or uncooked	10 oz.	284 g
Grated Edam or Gouda cheese	1 cup	250 mL
Green onions, sliced	8	8
Mayonnaise	1 cup	250 mL
Sour cream	1 cup	250 mL
Granulated sugar	2 tbsp.	30 mL
Grated medium Cheddar cheese	1 cup	250 mL
Bacon slices, cooked and crumbled	4 - 6	4 - 6

Cook macaroni in boiling water, cooking oil and salt in uncovered Dutch oven until tender but firm, about 5 to 7 minutes. Drain. Rinse with cold water. Drain well. Return macaroni to pot.

Add olive oil. Toss to coat.

Cut or break lettuce into small pieces. Spread in 9 × 13 inch (22 × 33 cm) pan. A large salad bowl may be used to get the full benefit of the pretty layers although it is more difficult to reach to the bottom so as to ensure getting some of every layer in each serving. If bowl is large enough, salad may be tossed just before serving.

To the lettuce, add layers of macaroni, ham, eggs, peas, Edam cheese and onion.

Mix mayonnaise, sour cream and sugar together. Spread over top, sealing right to the edge.

Sprinkle with Cheddar cheese then with bacon. Cover tightly with plastic wrap. Chill for 24 hours before serving. Serves 10 to 12.

The zesty flavor comes from the addition of several herbs. If you are tired of bland salads, this is for you. Most agreeable.

Pasta bows	8 oz.	250 g
Boiling water	2½ qts.	3 L
Cooking oil (optional)	1 tbsp.	15 mL
Salt	2 tsp.	10 mL
Cooking oil	½ cup	125 mL
Vinegar	⅓ cup	75 mL
Basil	2 tsp.	10 mL
Oregano	1 tsp.	5 mL
Garlic clove, minced	1	1
Chopped green onion	½ cup	125 mL
Grated Parmesan cheese	⅓ cup	75 mL
Parsley flakes	2 tsp.	10 mL
Salt	½ tsp.	2 mL
Pepper	¼ tsp.	1 mL
Cooked peas	¼ cup	60 mL
Cubed medium Cheddar cheese	½ cup	125 mL

Cook bows in boiling water, first amounts of cooking oil and salt in uncovered Dutch oven until tender but firm, about 14 to 16 minutes. Drain. Rinse with cold water. Drain well. Return bows to pot.

Mix next 10 ingredients together in a small bowl. Add to pasta. Toss well.

Add peas and Cheddar cheese. Toss. Cover and chill about 4 hours. Stir thorcughly from bottom. Transfer to bowl and serve. Makes about 5½ cups (1.25 L).

Note: You can also use tiny pasta shells in this salad. Use about 2 cups (500 mL) to equal 8 oz. (250 g) bows.

Pictured on page 71.

He is tired of being a fireman. He is always being told to go to blazes.

NOODLE SALAD

A moist salad with lots of color. A favorite.

Medium egg noodles	1 lb.	500 g
Boiling water	4 qts.	5 L
Cooking oil (optional)	1 tbsp.	15 mL
Salt	1 tbsp.	15 mL
Finely chopped onion	⅓ cup	75 mL
Grated carrot	½ cup	125 mL
Chopped celery	½ cup	125 mL
Green pepper, diced	1	1
Golden Italian salad dressing	1½ cups	375 mL
Club House Salad Supreme spice (or Spice Supreme, below)	1 tbsp.	15 mL

Cook noodles in boiling water, cooking oil and salt in uncovered Dutch oven until tender but firm, about 5 to 7 minutes. Drain. Rinse with cold water. Drain well.

Add onion, carrot, celery and green pepper. Toss.

Add salad dressing and spice. Toss well. Add as much spice as you like, even several spoonfuls. Go by taste. Makes about 7 cups (1.7 L).

SPICE SUPREME

Grated Romano cheese	2 tsp.	10 mL
Paprika	1½ tsp.	7 mL
Celery seed	1 tsp.	5 mL
Sesame seeds	½ tsp.	2 mL
Salt	½ tsp.	2 mL
Celery salt	¼ tsp.	1 mL
Turmeric	¼ tsp.	1 mL
Garlic powder	¼ tsp.	1 mL

Mix all ingredients together in small bowl. It is very easy to increase recipe so you can fill a small bottle. Makes 2 tbsp. (30 mL).

Paré Pointer

Is a trifle a three-barrelled rifle?

OLD FASHIONED PASTA SALAD

The addition of lettuce and chopped eggs makes this crunchy good.

Fusilli (FOOZ-ee-lee) pasta, 3 colors	8 oz.	250 g
Boiling water	2½ qts.	3 L
Cooking oil (optional)	1 tbsp.	15 mL
Salt	2 tsp.	10 mL
Chopped lettuce, lightly packed	4 cups	1 L
Hard-boiled eggs, chopped	3	3
Diced celery	¼ cup	60 mL
Sliced radishes	¼ cup	60 mL
Parsley flakes	2 tsp.	10 mL
Onion powder	½ tsp.	2 mL
Salt	½ tsp.	2 mL
Pepper	⅛ tsp.	0.5 mL
DRESSING		
Salad dressing (such as Miracle Whip)	1 cup	250 mL
Prepared mustard	1 tsp.	5 mL
Granulated sugar	1 tsp.	5 mL

Cook fusilli in boiling water, cooking oil and first amount of salt in uncovered Dutch oven until tender but firm, about 8 to 10 minutes. Drain. Rinse with cold water. Drain. Return fusilli to pot.

Add next 8 ingredients. Stir to mix.

Dressing: Mix salad dressing, mustard and sugar together. Add to salad and toss together well. Transfer to serving bowl. Makes about 8 cups (2 L).

Pictured on page 143.

Paré Pointer

His mother must be a chicken because he's such a cluck.

ORIENTAL PASTA SALAD

Fantastic flavor with or without shrimp.

Medium egg noodles	8 oz.	250 g
Boiling water	2½ qts.	3 L
Cooking oil (optional)	1 tbsp.	15 mL
Salt	2 tsp.	10 mL
Sliced fresh mushrooms	1 cup	250 mL
Green onions, chopped	2 - 3	2 - 3
Bean sprouts, large handful	1	1
Grated cabbage	1 cup	250 mL
Sliced cucumber, peeled or not	1 cup	250 mL
Sliced radishes	½ cup	125 mL
Grated carrot	¼ cup	60 mL
Small shrimp, canned or fresh cooked (optional)	1 cup	250 mL

DRESSING		
Hot water	2 tbsp.	30 mL
Chicken bouillon powder	1 tbsp.	15 mL
Soy sauce	3 tbsp.	50 mL
White vinegar	3 tbsp.	50 mL
Cooking oil	¼ cup	60 mL
Granulated sugar	2 tsp.	10 mL
Salt	½ tsp.	2 mL
Pepper	⅛ tsp.	0.5 mL

Cook noodles in boiling water, cooking oil and salt in uncovered Dutch oven until tender but firm, about 5 to 7 minutes. Drain. Rinse with cold water. Drain well. Return noodles to pot.

Combine next 8 ingredients with noodles.

Dressing: In small bowl, mix hot water with bouillon powder. Add remaining ingredients. Whisk well. Pour over noodle mixture. Toss. Put into bowl. Serves 8 as a side salad or 4 as a main course.

CHICKEN PASTA SALAD

A good mixture. Cucumber adds a nice flavor and some crunch as well. Mild.

Wagon wheels or other pasta	8 oz.	250 g
Boiling water	2½ qts.	3 L
Cooking oil (optional)	1 tbsp.	15 mL
Salt	2 tsp.	10 mL

(continued on next page)

Cooked peas	2 cups	500 mL
Cooked chicken, diced	1 cup	250 mL
Peeled, seeded and diced cucumber	½ cup	125 mL
DRESSING		
Salad dressing (such as Miracle Whip)	½ cup	125 mL
Vinegar	1 tsp.	5 mL
Seasoned salt	¾ tsp.	4 mL

Cook pasta in boiling water, cooking oil and salt in uncovered Dutch oven until tender but firm, about 5 to 7 minutes. Drain. Rinse with cold water. Drain well. Return pasta to pot.

Add peas, chicken and cucumber. Mix.

Dressing: Mix salad dressing, vinegar and seasoned salt together. Add to pasta mixture. Toss to coat. Makes about 6⅔ cups (1.6 L).

CRAB SEAFOOD SALAD

Easy to make. Serve in a lettuce cup for added color.

Tiny pasta shells	2 cups	500 mL
Boiling water	2½ qts.	3 L
Cooking oil (optional)	1 tbsp.	15 mL
Salt	2 tsp.	10 mL
Salad dressing (such as Miracle Whip)	¾ cup	175 mL
Chili sauce	1 tbsp.	15 mL
Lemon juice	1 tsp.	5 mL
Worcestershire sauce	½ tsp.	2 mL
Onion powder	¼ tsp.	1 mL
Salt	¼ tsp.	1 mL
Canned crab, cartilage removed	4 oz.	113 g
Chopped fresh parsley	¼ cup	60 mL
Paprika, sprinkle		

Cook shells in boiling water, cooking oil and first amount of salt in uncovered Dutch oven until tender but firm, about 8 to 11 minutes. Drain. Rinse with cold water. Drain well. Return shells to pot.

Combine salad dressing, chili sauce, lemon juice, Worcestershire sauce, onion powder and second amount of salt in small bowl. Pour over pasta. Toss well.

Add crab and parsley. Toss lightly. Put into pretty bowl. Sprinkle with paprika. Makes about 3¼ cups (750 mL).

FAR EAST TUNA SALAD

Easy to prepare. A nice crunch to it and economical as well.

Fine egg noodles	8 oz.	250 g
Boiling water	2½ qts.	3 L
Cooking oil (optional)	1 tbsp.	15 mL
Salt	2 tsp.	10 mL
Grated cabbage	1 cup	250 mL
Chunk tuna, drained and broken up	7 oz.	198 g
Green onions, chopped	2 - 3	2 - 3
DRESSING		
Cooking oil	½ cup	125 mL
Vinegar	3 tbsp.	50 mL
Chicken bouillon powder	1 tbsp.	15 mL
Granulated sugar	1 tbsp.	15 mL
Salt	½ tsp.	2 mL
Pepper	¼ tsp.	1 mL

Sprig of fresh dill, for garnish

Cook noodles in boiling water, cooking oil and salt in uncovered Dutch oven until tender but firm, about 4 to 6 minutes. Drain. Rinse with cold water. Drain well. Return noodles to pot.

Add cabbage, tuna and onion.

Dressing: Mix all ingredients together. Stir well. Pour over salad mixture. Toss well. Serve in bowl.

Garnish with fresh dill. Makes about 5½ cups (1.4 L).

Pictured on page 89.

PASTA COLE SLAW

Macaroni and cabbage dressed in a creamy sauce. Good.

Elbow macaroni	2 cups	500 mL
Boiling water	2½ qts.	3 L
Cooking oil (optional)	1 tbsp.	15 mL
Salt	2 tsp.	10 mL
Grated cabbage	2 cups	500 mL
Medium carrot, grated	1	1
Chopped green onion	¼ cup	60 mL
Salt	½ tsp.	2 mL

(continued on next page)

DRESSING

Salad dressing (such as Miracle Whip)	¾ cup	175 mL
Granulated sugar	¼ cup	60 mL
Vinegar	3 tbsp.	50 mL
Cooking oil	2 tbsp.	30 mL
Finely chopped onion	1 tbsp.	15 mL
Salt	1 tsp.	5 mL

Cook macaroni in boiling water, cooking oil and first amount of salt in uncovered Dutch oven until tender but firm, about 5 to 7 minutes. Drain. Rinse with cold water. Drain well. Return macaroni to pot.

Add cabbage, carrot, onion and second amount of salt. Mix.

Dressing: Put all ingredients into blender. Blend until smooth. Pour over salad. Toss. Transfer to serving bowl. Makes about 5½ cups (1.25 L) salad.

FRESH PLAIN PASTA

No eggs in this pasta.

All-purpose flour	2 cups	450 mL
Olive oil (or cooking oil)	2 tbsp.	30 mL
Water	¼ cup	60 mL

Mix all ingredients together. Dough should be stiff. Add more water or more flour as required. Roll out paper thin. Cut into short wide strips or long narrow strips. For noodles, roll up as for jelly roll and slice thinly. Boil in boiling salted water for 4 to 8 minutes until tender but firm, depending upon thickness. Serves 4.

WON TON WRAPPERS: Cut rolled dough into 3 inch (7.5 cm) squares.

EGG ROLL WRAPPERS: Cut rolled dough into 8 inch (20 cm) squares.

WHOLE WHEAT PASTA: In any one of the fresh pasta recipes in this book, use whole wheat flour instead of all-purpose flour. Using half whole wheat and half all-purpose flour makes a more tender product.

BEEF PASTA SALAD

Add leftover beef to pasta and vegetables and dress with a nippy dressing.

Spiral egg noodles, 3 colors	8 oz.	250 g
Boiling water	2½ qts.	3 L
Cooking oil (optional)	1 tbsp.	15 mL
Salt	2 tsp.	10 mL
Medium carrots, thinly sliced and cooked tender-crisp	2	2
Cooked roast beef, cut in thin strips	1½ cups	375 mL
Celery rib, sliced	1	1
DRESSING		
Sour cream	½ cup	125 mL
Red wine vinegar	2 tbsp.	30 mL
Cooking oil	2 tbsp.	30 mL
Horseradish	2 tsp.	10 mL
Salt	1 tsp.	5 mL
Pepper	⅛ tsp.	0.5 mL

Cook noodles in boiling water, cooking oil and salt in uncovered Dutch oven until tender but firm, about 5 to 7 minutes. Drain. Rinse with cold water. Drain. Return noodles to pot.

Add carrot, beef and celery. Stir.

Dressing: Mix remaining ingredients together. Add to salad and toss together to coat. Makes about 6 cups (1.5 L) salad.

FRESH EGG NOODLES

Extra liquid comes from eggs rather than water in this recipe.

All-purpose flour	2 cups	450 mL
Eggs	4	4
Olive oil (or cooking oil)	1 tbsp.	15 mL

Mix all together well. Knead until smooth. Roll paper thin. Cut into strips. This is easier if rolled like a jelly roll and sliced. Cook in boiling salted water, about 4 to 8 minutes depending on thickness, until tender but firm. Makes 1 pound (454 g). Serves 4.

WON TON WRAPPERS: Cut rolled dough into 3 inch (7.5 cm) squares.

EGG ROLL WRAPPERS: Cut rolled dough into 8 inch (20 cm) squares.

This may be used as noodles, or use large squares as manicotti or lasagne layers.

All-purpose flour	2 cups	450 mL
Eggs	2	2
Olive oil (or cooking oil)	2 tbsp.	30 mL
Water	2 - 4 tbsp.	30 - 60 mL

Measure flour into bowl. Make a well in center.

In small bowl beat eggs, olive oil and smallest amount of water with spoon. Slowly add to well while stirring. If too dry add more water. If too wet, simply add more flour. It won't hurt the pasta. Knead until smooth. Roll out paper thin. To make noodles, roll up dough like a jelly roll. Cut into thin slices. Unroll and you have noodles. Boil in lots of salted water until tender but firm, about 4 to 8 minutes depending on thickness. Makes 1 pound (454 g). Serves 4.

GREEN PASTA: Omit water. Add about ¼ cup (60 mL) cooked puréed or finely chopped spinach. If dough is sticky, add more flour. If too dry add a bit of water.

RED PASTA: Omit water. Add about ¼ cup (60 mL) cooked puréed beets. Add flour if dough is sticky. If too dry add a bit of water.

ORANGE PASTA: Omit water. Add up to ¼ cup (60 mL) tomato paste. Use more flour as needed. If too dry add a bit of water.

YELLOW PASTA: Omit Water. Add about ¼ cup (60 mL) cooked puréed carrots. Add flour if needed. If too dry add a bit of water. You can also leave water in recipe, omit carrots and add a pinch of saffron.

WON TON WRAPPERS: Cut rolled dough into 3 inch (7.5 cm) squares.

EGG ROLL WRAPPERS: Cut rolled dough into 8 inch (20 cm) squares.

Paré Pointer

You might think clocks are shy the way they cover their face with their hands.

BOLOGNESE SAUCE

This ragu sauce is a good version of the real thing.

Bacon slices, diced	2	2
Finely chopped onion	1 cup	250 mL
Finely chopped celery	½ cup	125 mL
Grated carrot	½ cup	125 mL
Lean ground beef	1½ lbs.	750 g
Milk	1 cup	250 mL
Butter	2 tbsp.	30 mL
Salt	1 tsp.	5 mL
Pepper	¼ tsp.	1 mL
Nutmeg	⅛ tsp.	0.5 mL
Canned tomatoes, broken up	14 oz.	398 mL
White wine (or use alcohol-free wine)	2 tbsp.	30 mL

Sauté bacon, onion, celery and carrot in frying pan until onion is clear.

Add ground beef. Scramble-fry just until no pink remains in meat.

Add milk, butter, salt, pepper and nutmeg. Simmer, stirring often, until most of the moisture has evaporated, about 30 minutes.

Add tomatoes and wine. Cover. Simmer slowly for about 30 minutes more. Stir occasionally. Makes 4 cups (900 ml).

1. Gnocchi page 110
2. Super Sauce page 39
3. Pasta And Eggs page 63
4. Tomato Zucchini Pasta page 58

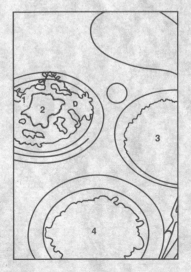

RED PEPPER SAUCE

Milky-red in color, this sauce is guaranteed to please. You may want to try only half the thickening if you like it quite thin. Mild.

Large red pepper, chopped	1	1
Chopped onion	½ cup	125 mL
Butter or margarine	2 tbsp.	30 mL
Light cream	1 cup	250 mL
Salt	¼ tsp.	1 mL
Cornstarch	2 tsp.	10 mL
Water	1 tbsp.	15 mL

Sauté red pepper and onion in butter until soft. Run through blender to smooth.

Heat cream and salt in saucepan until boiling. Stir occasionally.

Mix cornstarch into water. Stir into boiling cream to thicken. Add pepper-onion mixture. Stir. Serve over plates of pasta. Makes about 1¼ cups (275 mL) which will cover 8 oz. (250 g) of pasta.

MARINARA SAUCE

One of the well known pasta sauces. Red and spicy.

Olive oil (or cooking oil)	2 tbsp.	30 mL
Chopped onion	1 cup	250 mL
Garlic cloves, minced	2 - 3	2 - 3
Canned tomatoes, broken up	28 oz.	796 mL
Tomato paste	5½ oz.	156 mL
Granulated sugar	1 tbsp.	15 mL
Parsley flakes	2 tsp.	10 mL
Basil	1½ tsp.	7 mL
Oregano	½ tsp.	2 mL
Salt	½ tsp.	2 mL

Heat olive oil in frying pan. Add onion and garlic. Sauté until soft, about 5 minutes.

Add tomatoes, tomato paste, sugar, parsley flakes, basil, oregano and salt. Mix together. Bring to a boil. Stir occasionally as it simmers uncovered for about 15 minutes. Makes about 2⅔ cups (600 mL).

TOMATO SAUCE

This is the sauce to make when it is more convenient to use canned tomatoes rather than fresh. Makes a good all-round sauce.

Cooking oil	2 tbsp.	30 mL
Finely chopped onion	1½ cups	375 mL
Garlic clove, minced	1	1
Canned tomatoes, mashed	2 x 19 oz.	2 x 540 mL
Tomato sauce	7½ oz.	213 mL
Parsley flakes	1 tbsp.	15 mL
Granulated sugar	1 tbsp.	15 mL
Salt	1½ tsp.	7 mL
Seasoned salt	1½ tsp.	7 mL
Pepper	¼ tsp.	1 mL
Oregano	1 tsp.	5 mL
Basil	1 tsp.	5 mL

Heat cooking oil in Dutch oven over medium heat. Add onion and garlic. Saute until soft, about 5 minutes.

Add remaining ingredients. Stir. Bring to a boil. Boil uncovered. Stir occasionally for about 1 hour until desired consistency. Makes about 4 cups (900 mL).

TOMATO SALSA SAUCE

Make lots of this when tomato crops are plentiful. Freeze in cartons to always have on hand. Use for spaghetti sauce and also for pizza sauce.

Chopped onion	1 cup	250 mL
Finely chopped garlic (or to taste)	1 tbsp.	15 mL
Olive oil (or cooking oil)	3 tbsp.	50 mL
Tomatoes, peeled and coarsely chopped, with juice	5 cups	1.13 L
Tomato paste	5½ oz.	156 mL
Bay leaves	2 - 3	2 - 3
Basil	1½ tsp.	7 mL
Oregano	1½ tsp.	7 mL
Granulated sugar	2 tsp.	10 mL
Salt	1½ tsp.	7 mL
Pepper	½ tsp.	2 mL

(continued on next page)

Sauté onion and garlic in olive oil in large saucepan until soft.

Immerse tomatoes 1 or 2 at a time in boiling water for about 1 minute or until skin peels easily. Peel and chop. Add to saucepan. Add remaining ingredients. Stir. Bring to a boil. Allow to simmer uncovered until it reaches desired consistency, about 1¼ to 2 hours. Stir occasionally. Discard bay leaves. Makes about 2¾ cups (625 mL).

SUPER SAUCE: Scramble-fry 1 lb. (500 g) lean ground beef. Sprinkle with ½ tsp. (2 mL) salt. Add to Tomato Salsa Sauce. Makes a generous 4 cups (1 L).

Pictured on page 35.

CHILI NOODLES

The addition of chili powder and cheese makes a pleasant change.

Noodles, medium or broad	8 oz.	250 g
Boiling water	2½ qts.	3 L
Cooking oil (optional)	1 tbsp.	15 mL
Salt	2 tsp.	10 mL
Chili powder	1 tbsp.	15 mL
Butter or margarine, cut up	1 tbsp.	15 mL
Grated medium Cheddar cheese	1 cup	250 mL
Butter or margarine	2 tbsp.	30 mL
All-purpose flour	2 tbsp.	30 mL
Salt	½ tsp.	2 mL
Milk	2 cups	500 mL

Paprika, sprinkle

In large uncovered saucepan cook noodles in boiling water, cooking oil and first amount of salt until tender but firm, about 5 to 7 minutes. Drain. Return noodles to pot.

Add chili powder, first amount of butter and cheese. Stir until butter melts. Put into greased 1 quart (1 L) casserole.

Melt remaining butter in saucepan. Mix in flour and second amount of salt. Stir in milk until it boils and thickens. Sauce will be fairly thin. Pour over noodles.

Sprinkle with paprika. Bake uncovered in 350°F (180°C) oven for about 40 minutes. Served as is, it will have a light colored topping. When stirred it will have a darker color throughout. Serves 4.

MACARONI AND CHEESE

An old standby. Topping is optional. Creamy and cheesy.

Elbow macaroni	2 cups	500 mL
Boiling water	2½ qts.	3 L
Cooking oil (optional)	1 tbsp.	15 mL
Salt	2 tsp.	10 mL
Chopped onion	½ cup	125 mL
Butter or margarine	⅓ cup	75 mL
All-purpose flour	3 tbsp.	50 mL
Salt	½ tsp.	2 mL
Pepper	⅛ tsp.	0.5 mL
Paprika	¼ tsp.	1 mL
Milk	2¼ cups	550 mL
Grated medium Cheddar cheese	2 cups	500 mL
Dry bread crumbs	½ cup	125 mL
Butter or margarine, melted	2 tbsp.	30 mL

In large uncovered saucepan cook macaroni in boiling water, cooking oil and first amount of salt until tender but firm, about 5 to 7 minutes. Drain.

Sauté onion in butter in large saucepan until clear and soft.

Sprinkle onion with flour, second amount of salt, pepper and paprika. Mix. Stir in milk and cheese until it boils and thickens and cheese melts. Add macaroni. Stir. Turn into greased 2 quart (2 L) casserole.

This may be baked uncovered at this point without the topping. To bake with the topping, mix bread crumbs with melted butter, scatter over top and bake uncovered in 350°F (180°C) oven for about 30 minutes until hot. Serves 4 to 6.

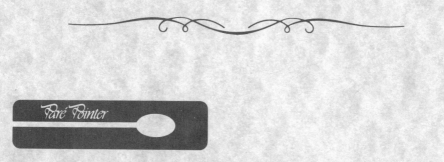

Paré Pointer

The teacher would only have six pupils in her schoolroom. She wanted her area to have a little class.

A puffy soufflé-like topping covers this pasta. Different and good.

Macaroni, or short spaghetti	1½ cups	375 mL
Boiling water	2 qts.	2 L
Cooking oil (optional)	2 tsp.	10 mL
Salt	2 tsp.	10 mL
Milk	2 cups	500 mL
Grated medium Cheddar cheese	1½ cups	375 mL
Butter or margarine	¼ cup	60 mL
Egg yolks, fork beaten	4	4
Water	2 tbsp.	30 mL
Hot milk mixture from saucepan		
Dry bread crumbs	1 cup	250 mL
Dry onion flakes	1 tbsp.	15 mL
Chopped pimiento	¼ cup	60 mL
Parsley flakes	1 tsp.	5 mL
Salt	1 tsp.	5 mL
Pepper	⅛ tsp.	0.5 mL
Egg whites, room temperature	4	4
Cream of tartar	¼ tsp.	1 mL

In large uncovered saucepan cook macaroni in boiling water, cooking oil and first amount of salt until tender but firm, about 5 to 7 minutes. Drain. Cool.

Put milk, cheese and butter into large saucepan. Heat and stir to melt cheese.

Beat egg yolks and water together. Add a little hot milk to it. Mix well. Pour this back into milk mixture in saucepan. Heat and stir to just below boiling. Remove from heat.

Add next 6 ingredients to saucepan. Stir. Add pasta. Mix together.

Beat egg whites and cream of tartar until stiff. Fold into pasta mixture. Turn into ungreased 2 quart (2.5 L) casserole. Bake uncovered in 325°F (160°C) oven for about 50 to 60 minutes until set and browned. Serves 6 to 8.

NOODLES ROMANOFF

With cottage cheese, sour cream and spices, this is a simple casserole to make. Either cheese topping is good.

Broad egg noodles	8 oz.	250 g
Boiling water	2½ qts.	3 L
Cooking oil (optional)	1 tbsp.	15 mL
Salt	2 tsp.	10 mL
Cottage cheese	1½ cups	375 mL
Sour cream	1 cup	250 mL
Green onions, chopped	8	8
Parsley flakes	1 tsp.	5 mL
Worcestershire sauce	1 tsp.	5 mL
Garlic salt	¼ tsp.	1 mL
Salt	½ tsp.	2 mL
Pepper	⅛ tsp.	0.5 mL
Grated medium Cheddar or Parmesan cheese	½ cup	125 mL

In large uncovered saucepan cook noodles in boiling water, cooking oil and first amount of salt until tender but firm, about 5 to 7 minutes. Drain. Return noodles to pot.

Mix next 8 ingredients together. Add to drained noodles. Stir. Put into 2 quart (2.5 L) greased casserole.

Sprinkle cheese over top. Bake covered in 350°F (180°C) oven for about 30 minutes. Serves 4.

VERM A PUFF

A light creamy colored casserole of noodles.

Vermicelli	10 oz.	284 g
Boiling water	3 qts.	4 L
Cooking oil (optional)	1 tbsp.	15 mL
Salt	1 tbsp.	15 mL
Egg whites, room temperature	3	3
Egg yolks	3	3
Butter or margarine, melted	½ cup	125 mL
Cottage cheese	1 cup	250 mL
Sour cream	1 cup	250 mL
Granulated sugar	1 tsp.	5 mL
Seasoned salt	1 tsp.	5 mL

(continued on next page)

In uncovered Dutch oven cook vermicelli in boiling water, cooking oil and salt until tender but firm, about 4 to 6 minutes. Drain.

Beat egg whites in bowl until stiff. Set aside.

With same beater, beat egg yolks in large bowl until frothy. Add butter, cottage cheese, sour cream, sugar and seasoned salt. Mix together. Add noodles and stir. Fold egg whites into noodle mixture. Turn into greased 2 quart (2.5 L) casserole. Bake uncovered in 375°F (190°C) oven for about 40 minutes. Casserole will test done if you insert a knife and it comes out clean. Serves 6.

Pictured on page 17.

CREAMY PARMESAN NOODLES

Quick and easy. Simply toss noodles in a creamy sauce.

Medium egg noodles	8 oz.	250 g
Boiling water	2½ qts.	3 L
Cooking oil (optional)	1 tbsp.	15 mL
Salt	2 tsp.	10 mL
Butter or margarine	¼ cup	60 mL
All-purpose flour	¼ cup	60 mL
Chicken bouillon powder	4 tsp.	20 mL
Milk	2 cups	500 mL
Grated Parmesan cheese	¼ cup	60 mL
Chopped fresh parsley	1-2 tbsp.	15-30 mL
Salt, sprinkle (optional)		
Paprika, sprinkle		

In large uncovered saucepan cook noodles in boiling water, cooking oil and first amount of salt until tender but firm, about 5 to 7 minutes. Drain. Return noodles to pot.

Meanwhile, melt butter in small saucepan. Mix in flour and bouillon powder. Stir in milk until it boils and thickens.

Add cheese and parsley to milk sauce. Stir. Add to drained pasta. Toss well. Taste for salt. You may want to add some.

Turn onto warm platter. Sprinkle with paprika. Serve. Makes 4 cups (1 L) creamy noodles.

NOODLES WITH A CRUNCH

Nutty and crunchy. A good combination. This is an ideal way to use left-over noodles.

Spaghetti	8 oz.	250 g
Boiling water	2½ qts.	3 L
Cooking oil (optional)	1 tbsp.	15 mL
Salt	2 tsp.	10 mL
Slivered almonds	½ cup	125 mL
Butter or margarine	1 tbsp.	15 mL
Butter or margarine	3 tbsp.	50 mL
Chopped fresh parsley	¼ cup	60 mL
Poppy seeds	1 tbsp.	15 mL

Cook spaghetti in boiling water, cooking oil and salt in large uncovered saucepan until tender but firm, about 11 to 13 minutes. Drain.

Sauté almonds in first amount of butter in large pot or frying pan until brown.

Add remaining butter, parsley and poppy seeds. Add spaghetti and toss together. Makes 5 cups (1.25 L).

NIPPY NOODLES

Green-flecked sauced noodles with a bit of nip.

Egg noodles, medium or broad	8 oz.	250 g
Boiling water	2½ qts.	3 L
Cooking oil (optional)	1 tbsp.	15 mL
Salt	2 tsp.	10 mL
Butter or margarine	¼ cup	60 mL
Finely chopped green onion	¼ cup	60 mL
Finely chopped onion	¼ cup	60 mL
Garlic clove, minced	1	1
Sour cream	1 cup	250 mL
Worcestershire sauce	2 tbsp.	30 mL
Parsley flakes	1 tsp.	5 mL
Pepper	½ tsp.	2 mL
Grated Parmesan cheese, heavy sprinkle		

(continued on next page)

Rigatoni Broccoli Bake

- Rigatoni - 250 g / 8 oz.
- Boiling water - 3 L
- Cooking oil (optional) - 1 tbsp
- Salt - 2 tsp
- Butter - ½ c.
- All-Pur. Flour - ⅓ c.
- Milk - 3 c.
- Grated Parm. 3¼ c
- Salt 1 tsp
- Garlic Salt ½ tsp

- Nutmeg ⅛ tsp
- Thyme ⅛ tsp
- Grated Sharp Cheddar 1½ c.
- Frsh. Broccoli, cut up 1½ lbs / 750 g
  (2 x 284 g froz. pack / 2 x 10 oz) cooked

In large uncovered saucepan cook noodles in boiling water, cooking oil and salt until tender but firm, about 5 to 7 minutes. Drain. Return noodles to pot.

Melt butter in frying pan. Add all onion and garlic. Sauté until soft.

Add sour cream, Worcestershire sauce, parsley and pepper. Heat and stir. Add sauce to noodles. Stir. Turn onto warm platter or plates.

Sprinkle with Parmesan cheese. Serves 4.

COTTAGE NOODLES

A delicious noodle dish. Cheddar cheese can be omitted for a tasty variation. Contains cottage cheese also.

Fine egg noodles	8 oz.	250 g
Boiling water	2½ qts.	3 L
Cooking oil (optional)	1 tbsp.	15 mL
Salt	2 tsp.	10 mL
Cottage cheese	2 cups	500 mL
Sour cream	1 cup	250 mL
Finely chopped onion	¼ cup	60 mL
Garlic clove, minced (optional)	1	1
Worcestershire sauce	1 tsp.	5 mL
Salt	¾ tsp.	4 mL
Pepper	¼ tsp.	1 mL
Grated medium Cheddar cheese	2 cups	500 mL

Paprika, sprinkle

In large uncovered saucepan cook noodles in boiling water, cooking oil and first amount of salt until tender but firm, about 4 to 6 minutes. Drain. Return noodles to pot.

Mix next 8 ingredients together. Add to pasta. Stir. Turn into 2½ to 3 quart (3 to 3.5 L) greased casserole.

Sprinkle with paprika. Bake uncovered in 350°F (180°C) oven for about 45 minutes. Serves 6 to 8.

CREAMED MACARONI

No cheese in this. Just creamy plain and just plain good.

Elbow macaroni	2 cups	500 mL
Boiling water	2½ qts.	3 L
Cooking oil (optional)	1 tbsp.	15 mL
Salt	2 tsp.	10 mL
Butter or margarine	¼ cup	60 mL
All-purpose flour	¼ cup	60 mL
Salt	½ tsp.	2 mL
Pepper	⅛ tsp.	0.5 mL
Milk	2 cups	500 mL
Butter or margarine	2 tbsp.	30 mL
Dry bread crumbs	½ cup	125 mL

In large uncovered saucepan cook macaroni in boiling water, cooking oil and first amount of salt until tender but firm, about 5 to 7 minutes. Drain. Return macaroni to pot.

Melt butter in medium saucepan. Mix in flour, second amount of salt and pepper. Stir in milk until it boils and thickens. Mix with macaroni and put into 2 quart (2 L) greased casserole.

Melt butter in small saucepan. Stir in crumbs. Scatter over top of macaroni. Bake uncovered in 350°F (180°C) oven for 25 to 30 minutes until browned and hot. Serves 6.

STOVE TOP MACARONI AND CHEESE

A snap to prepare. Good eating.

Elbow macaroni	2 cups	500 mL
Boiling water	2½ qts.	3 L
Cooking oil (optional)	1 tbsp.	15 mL
Salt	2 tsp.	10 mL
Milk	½ cup	125 mL
Butter or margarine	¼ cup	60 mL
Onion salt	1 tsp.	5 mL
Pepper (white is best)	⅛ tsp.	0.5 mL
Grated medium Cheddar cheese	2 cups	500 mL

(continued on next page)

In large uncovered saucepan cook macaroni in boiling water, cooking oil and salt until tender but firm, about 5 to 7 minutes. Drain. Return macaroni to pot.

Add remaining ingredients. Heat slowly, stirring to melt cheese and heat through. Serves 6.

CREAMY CHEEZY NOODLES

Try these creamy rich noodles.

Vermicelli	4 oz.	125 g
Boiling water	2 qts.	2.5 L
Cooking oil (optional)	2 tsp.	10 mL
Salt	2 tsp.	10 mL
Grated mozzarella cheese	1 cup	250 mL
Butter or margarine	2 tbsp.	30 mL
Whipping cream	¾ cup	175 mL
Salt, sprinkle		
Pepper, sprinkle		
Grated Parmesan cheese	½ cup	125 mL
Whipping cream	¼ cup	60 mL
Grated Parmesan cheese	¼ cup	60 mL

In large uncovered saucepan cook vermicelli in boiling water, cooking oil and first amount of salt until tender but firm, about 4 to 6 minutes. Drain. Return pasta to pot.

Add next 6 ingredients to pasta. Stir. Put into greased 1 quart (1 L) casserole.

Mix second amounts of cream and Parmesan cheese together. Spread over top. Bake uncovered in 350°F (180°C) oven for 25 to 35 minutes until hot and browned. Serves 4 to 6.

Paré Pointer

For their church they want a bell that will only sound off when it's tolled.

NUTTY CHEEZY LINGUINI

A nutty olive salad tops this pasta.

Chopped walnuts	½ cup	125 mL
Chopped fresh parsley	¼ cup	60 mL
Chopped pitted black olives	¼ cup	60 mL
Chopped pimiento	2 tbsp.	30 mL
Basil	½ tsp.	2 mL
Grated medium Cheddar cheese	1½ cups	375 mL
Linguini	1 lb.	500 g
Boiling water	4 qts.	5 L
Cooking oil (optional)	1 tbsp.	15 mL
Salt	1 tbsp.	15 mL
Butter or margarine, melted	¼ cup	60 mL
Seasoned salt	½ tsp.	2 mL

Mix first 6 ingredients together in bowl. Set aside.

In large uncovered Dutch oven cook linguini in boiling water, cooking oil and salt until tender but firm, about 11 to 13 minutes. Drain. Return linguini to pot.

Add butter and seasoned salt. Toss together. Divide among plates. Spoon nut-cheese mixture over plates of linguini. Serves 6 to 8.

NOODLE CURRY

A good curry-flavored noodle dish. Yellow in color.

Egg noodles, medium or broad	8 oz.	250 g
Boiling water	2½ qts.	3 L
Cooking oil (optional)	1 tbsp.	15 mL
Salt	2 tsp.	10 mL
Butter or margarine	3 tbsp.	50 mL
All-purpose flour	3 tbsp.	50 mL
Curry powder	1½ tsp.	7 mL
Salt	1 tsp.	5 mL
Pepper	¼ tsp.	1 mL
Milk	1½ cups	375 mL
Sour cream	½ cup	125 mL

(continued on next page)

In large uncovered saucepan or Dutch oven cook noodles in boiling water, cooking oil and first amount of salt until tender but firm, about 5 to 7 minutes. Drain. Return noodles to pot.

Melt butter in medium saucepan. Mix in flour, curry powder, second amount of salt and pepper. Stir in milk until it boils and thickens.

Stir in sour cream. Mix with noodles. May be served now or may be put into 2 quart (2 L) greased casserole and baked uncovered in 350°F (180°C) oven for 20 to 25 minutes until bubbly hot. Serves 4.

FETTUCCINE THAT'S CREAMY

Fabulous flavor. Creamy with a taste of bacon.

Fettuccine	**1 lb.**	**500 g**
Boiling water	**4 qts.**	**5 L**
Cooking oil (optional)	**1 tbsp.**	**15 mL**
Salt	**1 tbsp.**	**15 mL**
Butter or margarine, melted	**¼ cup**	**60 mL**
Salt	**1 tsp.**	**5 mL**
Pepper	**⅛ tsp.**	**0.5 mL**
Whipping cream	**1 cup**	**250 mL**
Velveeta cheese, cut up (or use mild, soft, process cheese)	**8 oz.**	**250 g**
Bacon slices, cooked and diced	**8**	**8**

Cook fettuccine in boiling water, cooking oil and first amount of salt in uncovered Dutch oven until tender but firm, about 5 to 7 minutes. Drain. Return to pot.

Add melted butter, second amount of salt and pepper. Toss and keep hot.

Meanwhile heat cream, cheese and bacon in saucepan until cheese is melted. Add to noodle mixture and toss. Makes about 8 cups (2 L).

Paré Pointer

You should treat a baby goat just like a kid.

CHEESELESS NOODLES

Very lightly spiced. Contains mushrooms. Delicate flavor.

Thinly sliced onion	2 cups	500 mL
Thinly sliced mushrooms	4 cups	1 L
Butter or margarine	¼ cup	60 mL
Vermicelli	1 lb.	500 g
Boiling water	4 qts.	5 L
Cooking oil (optional)	1 tbsp.	15 mL
Salt	1 tbsp.	15 mL
Whipping cream	2 cups	500 mL
Salt	1 tsp.	5 mL
Pepper, sprinkle		
Nutmeg, light sprinkle		

Sauté onion and mushrooms in butter until soft.

In uncovered Dutch oven cook vermicelli in boiling water, cooking oil and first amount of salt until tender but firm, about 4 to 6 minutes. Drain. Return vermicelli to pot.

Add cream, second amount of salt and pepper to mushroom-onion mixture. Sprinkle lightly with nutmeg, just barely enough to taste. Heat. Mix with noodles. Serves 8. Makes 12 cups (2.7 L).

PASTA CARBONARA

A bacon and egg pasta. Eggs are mixed into and cooked by the hot pasta. A popular choice. The Romans love this dish.

Spaghetti or linguini	10 oz.	325 g
Boiling water	3 qts.	4 L
Cooking oil (optional)	1 tbsp.	15 mL
Salt	1 tbsp.	15 mL
Bacon slices, cut cross-wise in narrow strips	1 cup	250 mL
Egg yolks	4	4
Whipping cream	2 tbsp.	30 mL
Grated Parmesan cheese	3 tbsp.	50 mL
Salt	½ tsp.	2 mL
Pepper	½ tsp.	2 mL
Grated Parmesan cheese		

(continued on next page)

Cook spaghetti in boiling water, cooking oil and first amount of salt in large uncovered saucepan until tender but firm, about 11 to 13 minutes. Drain.

In frying pan sauté bacon to cook. Drain off fat. Add spaghetti to bacon in pan. Stir to absorb flavor. Keep hot.

In heated bowl beat egg yolks until light. Mix in cream, first amount of Parmesan cheese, second amount of salt and pepper. Stir. Turn spaghetti and bacon into egg mixture. Stir immediately lifting from bottom. The hot pasta will cook the eggs as you stir.

Sprinkle with Parmesan cheese. Makes 2 platefuls.

CARBONARA PLUS: Sauté 1 cup (250 mL) chopped onion with the bacon and also 1 cup (250 mL) sliced fresh mushrooms. Add and toss before serving.

NOODLES CON QUESO

A good different pot of noodles. Very tasty. The red and green bits in a creamy sauce make noodles cahn-KAY-soh very colorful. To halve recipe, simply freeze leftover green chilies and pimiento.

Finely chopped green pepper	2 tbsp.	30 mL
Velveeta cheese (or use another mild, soft, process cheese)	8 oz.	250 g
Light cream	½ cup	125 mL
Chopped green chilies	4 oz.	114 mL
Chopped pimiento	2 tsp.	10 mL
Paprika	¼ tsp.	1 mL
Broad egg noodles	1 lb.	500 g
Boiling water	4 qts.	5 L
Cooking oil (optional)	1 tbsp.	15 mL
Salt	1 tbsp.	15 mL

Cook green pepper in small amount of water in medium saucepan until tender-crisp. Drain off water.

Add next 5 ingredients to green pepper. Heat slowly to melt cheese. Makes 1⅓ cups (300 mL) sauce.

In uncovered Dutch oven cook noodles in boiling water, cooking oil and salt until tender but firm, about 5 to 7 minutes. Drain. Add to sauce. Toss well. Makes a scant 7 cups (1.7 L).

NOODLES ALFREDO-STYLE

One of the quickest and easiest pasta plates.

Egg noodles, green, red or white	8 oz.	250 g
Boiling water	2½ qts.	3 L
Cooking oil (optional)	1 tbsp.	15 mL
Salt	2 tsp.	10 mL
Butter or margarine	¼ cup	60 mL
Grated Parmesan cheese	¼ cup	60 mL
(or use twice as much grated sharp Cheddar cheese)		
Salt, sprinkle (optional)		
Grated Parmesan cheese (or more grated Cheddar cheese), sprinkle		

In large uncovered saucepan cook noodles in boiling water, cooking oil and first amount of salt until tender but firm, about 5 to 7 minutes. Drain and return noodles to saucepan.

Add butter and first amount of Parmesan cheese. Heat and stir until butter is absorbed and cheese is fairly well melted. Taste for salt, adding a sprinkle if desired.

Serve with additional Parmesan cheese sprinkled over top or served on the side. If using Cheddar cheese with noodles, sprinkle with additional Cheddar cheese. Makes 3 cups (750 mL).

1. Spaghetti Pizza page 119
2. Spaghetti And Meatballs page 78
3. Beef Italia page 99

RIGATONI BROCCOLI BAKE

A nice and creamy dish. Green shows throughout. Good choice.

Rigatoni	8 oz.	250 g
Boiling water	2½ qts.	3 L
Cooking oil (optional)	1 tbsp.	15 mL
Salt	2 tsp.	10 mL
Butter or margarine	⅓ cup	75 mL
All-purpose flour	⅓ cup	75 mL
Milk	3 cups	700 mL
Grated Parmesan cheese	¾ cup	175 mL
Salt	1 tsp.	5 mL
Garlic salt	½ tsp.	2 mL
Nutmeg	⅛ tsp.	0.5 mL
Thyme	⅛ tsp.	0.5 mL
Grated sharp Cheddar cheese	1½ cups	350 mL
Fresh broccoli, cut up (or 2 x 10 oz., 2 x 284 g, frozen packages) cooked	1½ lbs.	750 g
Grated Swiss cheese	¾ cup	175 mL

Cook rigatoni in boiling water, cooking oil and first amount of salt in large uncovered saucepan until tender but firm, about 12 to 15 minutes.

Meanwhile, melt butter in saucepan. Mix in flour. Stir in milk until it boils and thickens.

Add Parmesan cheese, second amount of salt, garlic salt, nutmeg, thyme and Cheddar cheese. Stir.

Drain rigatoni. Return pasta to pot. Add cheese sauce and cooked broccoli. Mix well. Pour into greased 9 x 13 inch (22 x 33 cm) pan.

Sprinkle with Swiss cheese. Bake uncovered in 350°F (180°C) oven to melt cheese, about 20 minutes. Serves 12 oversize or 15 average pieces to your favorite crowd.

Pictured on page 17.

Paré Pointer

Forbidden fruit is said to taste sweeter. Too bad it spoils faster.

55

TOMATO SAUCED MACARONI

A good combination of convenience foods.

Macaroni	3 cups	750 mL
Boiling water	3 qts.	4 L
Cooking oil (optional)	1 tbsp.	15 mL
Salt	1 tbsp.	15 mL
Canned tomatoes, mashed	19 oz.	540 mL
Grated medium Cheddar cheese	1 cup	250 mL
Condensed cream of mushroom soup	10 oz.	284 mL
Chicken bouillon powder	2 tsp.	10 mL
Salt	½ tsp.	2 mL
Pepper	¼ tsp.	1 mL

In uncovered Dutch oven cook macaroni in boiling water, cooking oil and first amount of salt until tender but firm, about 5 to 7 minutes. Drain.

Meanwhile heat remaining ingredients in saucepan. Mix macaroni with sauce. Serve. Makes 7 cups (1.6 L).

PRIMAVERA STYLE NOODLES

This excellent flavored dish is full of brightly colored vegetables. Fantastic.

Olive oil (or cooking oil)	2 tbsp.	30 mL
Carrots, cut in matchsticks or coin shapes	1 cup	250 mL
Chopped onion	1 cup	250 mL
Medium zucchini, with peel, cut bite size	1	1
Broccoli flowerettes	1 cup	250 mL
Seasoned salt	1 tsp.	5 mL
Basil	½ tsp.	2 mL
Whole mushrooms, drained	10 oz.	284 mL
Broad egg noodles	8 oz.	250 g
Boiling water	2½ qts.	3 L
Cooking oil (optional)	1 tbsp.	15 mL
Salt	2 tsp.	10 mL
Grated Parmesan cheese	3 tbsp.	50 mL
Grated Parmesan cheese, sprinkle (optional)		

(continued on next page)

Heat olive oil in large frying pan or wok. Add carrot and onion. Sauté for about 5 minutes. Stir often until soft.

Add zucchini, broccoli, seasoned salt and basil. Sauté 5 minutes more stirring frequently.

Stir in mushrooms to heat through.

Cook noodles in boiling water, cooking oil and salt in large uncovered saucepan until tender but firm, about 5 to 7 minutes.

Drain noodles. Combine with vegetable mixture. Stir in first amount of Parmesan cheese. Turn into large serving bowl. Sprinkle with additional Parmesan cheese if desired. Serves 4.

SPECKLED PASTA

This good dish is crunchy and speckled. Different. Contains cabbage.

Chopped onion	1 cup	250 mL
Butter or margarine	¼ cup	60 mL
Coarsely grated cabbage	4 cups	1 L
Paprika	1 tsp.	5 mL
Salt	1 tsp.	5 mL
Pepper	¼ tsp.	1 mL
Broad egg noodles	8 oz.	250 g
Boiling water	2½ qts.	3 L
Cooking oil (optional)	1 tbsp.	15 mL
Salt	2 tsp.	10 mL
Sour cream	¼ cup	60 mL
Poppy seeds	2 tbsp.	30 mL
Grated Parmesan cheese	2 tbsp.	30 mL

Sauté onion in butter until soft.

Add cabbage, paprika, first amount of salt and pepper. Sauté slowly, covered, over low heat for about 10 minutes.

In large uncovered saucepan cook noodles in boiling water, cooking oil and second amount of salt until tender but firm, about 5 to 7 minutes. Drain. Return noodles to pot.

Add sour cream, poppy seeds and cheese. Heat. Pour onto noodles. Toss well. Makes 6 cups (1.5 L).

TOMATO ZUCCHINI PASTA

Lots of eye appeal to this appetizing dish.

Spaccatella (spac-ah-TELL-ah) or medium egg noodles	8 oz.	250 g
Boiling water	2½ qts.	3 L
Cooking oil (optional)	1 tbsp.	15 mL
Salt	2 tsp.	10 mL
Butter or margarine	½ cup	125 mL
Chopped onion	1 cup	250 mL
Green pepper, chopped	1	1
Sliced zucchini, with peel	5 cups	1.2 L
Cherry tomatoes, halved	12	12
Grated Gruyère cheese (or Swiss)	1 cup	250 mL
Grated Parmesan cheese	¾ cup	175 mL
Chopped fresh parsley	½ cup	125 mL
Salt	1 tsp.	5 mL

Fresh Parmesan cheese, grated, sprinkle

Cook pasta in boiling water, cooking oil and first amount of salt in un-covered large saucepan until tender but firm, about 5 to 7 minutes. Drain. Return pasta to pot.

Meanwhile, melt butter in large Dutch oven. Add onion and green pepper. Sauté until onions are clear.

Add zucchini, tomatoes, Gruyère cheese, first amount of Parmesan cheese, parsley and second amount of salt. Continue to sauté until cheese melts. Add to pasta. Stir.

Put into 3 quart (3.5 L) greased casserole. Sprinkle with remaining Parmesan cheese. Cover. Bake in 350°F (180°C) oven for 30 to 40 minutes. Serves 6.

Pictured on page 35.

Paré Pointer

You can tell they are halloween birds. They go "Twick tweet, twick tweet".

SPINACH NOODLE CASSEROLE

Different and delicious.

Egg noodles, medium or broad	12 oz.	375 g
Boiling water	3 qts.	4 L
Cooking oil (optional)	1 tbsp.	15 mL
Salt	1 tbsp.	15 mL
Lean ground beef	2 lbs.	1 kg
Chopped onion	1 cup	250 mL
Cooking oil	1 tbsp.	15 mL
Salt	1½ tsp.	7 mL
Pepper	¼ tsp.	1 mL
Tomato sauce	7½ oz.	213 mL
Tomato paste	5½ oz.	156 mL
Eggs, beaten	2	2
Milk	¼ cup	60 mL
Cottage cheese	2 cups	500 mL
Frozen chopped spinach, thawed	10 oz.	284 g
Nutmeg	⅛ tsp.	0.5 mL
Grated medium Cheddar cheese	1 cup	250 mL

In uncovered Dutch oven cook noodles in boiling water, first amounts of cooking oil and salt until tender but firm, about 5 to 7 minutes. Drain. Return noodles to pot.

Scramble-fry ground beef and onion in second amount of cooking oil until browned. Add second amount of salt and pepper.

Mix tomato sauce, tomato paste, eggs, milk, cottage cheese, spinach and nutmeg into drained pasta. Add meat mixture. Stir. Put into 3 quart (3.5 L) casserole.

Sprinkle with cheese. Bake covered in 350°F (180°C) oven for 20 minutes. Remove cover. Bake about 10 minutes more to brown a bit. Serves 8.

Be careful dealing with a sculptor. They are always chiselling.

QUICK FIX CASSEROLE

Asparagus and eggs are a natural go-together. Use packaged macaroni and cheese for real convenience.

Packaged macaroni and cheese dinner	7¼ oz.	200 g
Canned asparagus pieces, drained, reserve juice	10 oz.	284 mL
Hard-boiled eggs, sliced	3	3
Black pitted olives, sliced	8-10	8-10
Reserved asparagus juice		
Dry bread crumbs	¼ cup	60 mL
Grated medium Cheddar cheese	½ cup	125 mL

Prepare macaroni and cheese according to package directions. Put ⅔ of it into greased 1 quart (1 L) casserole.

Layer asparagus over top. Layer egg over asparagus. Scatter olives over eggs. Pour asparagus juice over all. Layer remaining ⅓ macaroni over top.

In small bowl, mix bread crumbs with cheese. Spread over macaroni. Bake uncovered in 350°F (180°C) oven for about 30 minutes. Serves 4.

VEGETABLE PASTA MIX

This is mixed with a light sauce. Contains no cheese but grated Parmesan may be sprinkled over before serving.

Spaghetti	8 oz.	250 g
Boiling water	2½ qts.	3 L
Cooking oil (optional)	1 tbsp.	15 mL
Salt	2 tsp.	10 mL
Frozen vegetable mixture, your favorite	2 cups	500 mL
Boiling salted water		
Water	¼ cup	60 mL
Cornstarch	2 tsp.	10 mL
Onion salt	½ tsp.	2 mL
Garlic salt	¼ tsp.	1 mL
Granulated sugar	2 tsp.	10 mL
Vinegar	2 tbsp.	30 mL
Tomatoes, cut in 6 wedges each	2	2
Chopped pecans or walnuts	2 tbsp.	30 mL

(continued on next page)

Cook spaghetti in first amount of boiling water, cooking oil and salt in large uncovered saucepan until tender but firm, about 11 to 13 minutes. Drain. Return spaghetti to pot.

In another saucepan cook vegetables in second amount of boiling salted water. Drain.

Mix next 6 ingredients in small saucepan. Bring to a boil, stirring to thicken.

Add tomatoes and nuts. Heat through. Add to drained spaghetti along with vegetables. Toss well. Serve immediately. Makes 5 cups (1.25 L).

GORGONZOLA FLORENTINE

If Gorgonzola is not readily available, Blue cheese may be used. Flavor is quite mild.

Fettuccine noodles	8 oz.	250 g
Boiling water	2½ qts.	3 L
Cooking oil (optional)	1 tbsp.	15 mL
Salt	2 tsp.	10 mL
Cottage cheese	½ cup	125 mL
Frozen chopped spinach, cooked according to package directions	10 oz.	284 g
Grated Parmesan cheese	¼ cup	60 mL
Onion powder	¼ tsp.	1 mL
Whipping cream	1 cup	250 mL
Gorgonzola cheese, cut up	3 oz.	85 g
Salt, sprinkle (optional)		
Pepper, sprinkle (optional)		
Grated Parmesan cheese		

Cook fettuccine in boiling water, cooking oil and first amount of salt in uncovered large saucepan until tender but firm, about 5 to 7 minutes. Drain. Return fettuccine to pot.

Stir next 4 ingredients into fettuccine in saucepan over low heat.

In small saucepan heat cream until it boils. Add Gorgonzola cheese. Stir to melt. Taste for salt and pepper, adding if needed. Turn noodle mixture out onto warm plates or platter. Pour sauce over top.

Sprinkle Parmesan cheese over top. Makes about 4½ cups (1.1 L).

RED HEAD PASTA

The red sauce is both colorful and tasty. It contains mushrooms, zucchini and green peppers.

Olive oil (or cooking oil)	1 tbsp.	15 mL
Sliced fresh mushrooms	1 cup	250 mL
Medium zucchini, with peel, sliced	1	1
Green pepper, cut in matchsticks	⅓ cup	75 mL
Canned tomatoes, mashed	14 oz.	398 mL
Tomato paste	5½ oz.	156 mL
Grated Parmesan cheese	⅓ cup	75 mL
Basil	¼ tsp.	1 mL
Salt	½ tsp.	2 mL
Pepper	⅛ tsp.	0.5 mL
Medium egg noodles	8 oz.	250 g
Boiling water	2½ qts.	3 L
Cooking oil (optional)	1 tbsp.	15 mL
Salt	2 tsp.	10 mL
Butter or margarine	1 - 2 tbsp.	15 - 30 mL
Grated Parmesan cheese		

Heat olive oil in frying pan. Add mushrooms, zucchini and green pepper. Sauté for 5 minutes.

Add tomatoes, tomato paste, first amount of Parmesan cheese, basil, first amount of salt and pepper. Cover and simmer slowly for 15 minutes.

Cook noodles in boiling water, cooking oil and second amount of salt in large uncovered saucepan until tender but firm, about 5 to 7 minutes.

Drain. Return noodles to pot. Stir in butter. Arrange on warm platter. Spoon sauce over pasta. Sprinkle with remaining Parmesan cheese. Serves 4.

Pare Pointer

Doctor Bell fell down the well and broke his collar bone. A doctor should attend the sick and leave the well alone.

Creamy pasta in a bowl with grated egg yolks on top surrounded with grated cheese.

Butter or margarine	¼ cup	60 mL
Chopped onion	½ cup	125 mL
All-purpose flour	¼ cup	60 mL
Salt	1 tsp.	5 mL
Pepper	¼ tsp.	1 mL
Paprika	¼ tsp.	1 mL
Milk	2 cups	500 mL
Chopped parsley	2 tbsp.	30 mL
Chopped pimiento	2 tbsp.	30 mL
Hard-boiled eggs, whites only, chopped	4	4
Grated medium Cheddar cheese	½ cup	125 mL
Short rigatoni or macaroni	2 cups	500 mL
Boiling water	2½ qts.	3 L
Cooking oil (optional)	1 tbsp.	15 mL
Salt	2 tsp.	10 mL
Hard-boiled eggs, yolks only, grated	4	4
Grated medium Cheddar cheese	½ cup	125 mL

Melt butter in saucepan. Add onion. Sauté until soft and clear.

Sprinkle flour, first amount of salt, pepper and paprika over top. Mix. Stir in milk until it boils and thickens.

Add parsley, pimiento, chopped egg whites and first amount of Cheddar cheese. Stir to melt cheese. Keep warm.

Cook rigatoni in boiling water, cooking oil and second amount of salt in uncovered Dutch oven until tender but firm, about 12 to 15 minutes. Drain. Combine with sauce. Put into serving bowl.

Arrange grated egg yolks over center of rigatoni and sauce or place in lines diagonally, side by side. Place remaining cheese around edge of yolks. Serves 4.

Pictured on page 35.

Paré Pointer

Gold soup is made with fourteen carrots.

MACARONI ZUCCHINI CASSEROLE

A great way to spike up a packaged meal. Contains cottage cheese and yogurt.

Packaged macaroni and cheese dinner	7¼ oz.	220 g
Chopped zucchini, with peel	2 cups	500 mL
Butter or margarine	2 tbsp.	30 mL
All-purpose flour	2 tsp.	10 mL
Cottage cheese	1 cup	250 mL
Yogurt	½ cup	125 mL
Oregano	½ tsp.	2 mL
Salt	½ tsp.	2 mL
Crushed cornflakes	½ cup	125 mL
Butter or margarine, melted	1 tbsp.	15 mL

Prepare macaroni and cheese according to package directions.

Sauté zucchini in first amount of butter until tender, about 4 to 5 minutes.

Sprinkle flour over zucchini. Mix in. Add cottage cheese, yogurt, oregano and salt. Add macaroni and cheese. Mix together. Turn into greased 2 quart (2.5 L) casserole.

Stir cornflakes into remaining melted butter. Spread over casserole. Bake uncovered in 350°F (180°C) oven for 30 to 40 minutes. Serves 4 to 6.

FETTUCCINE AND TOMATOES

What a scrumptious sight! Green fettuccine and red tomatoes.

Green fettuccine	12 oz.	375 g
Boiling water	3 qts.	4 L
Cooking oil (optional)	1 tbsp.	15 mL
Salt	1 tbsp.	15 mL
Chopped onion	½ cup	125 mL
Chopped celery	¼ cup	60 mL
Garlic cloves, minced	2	2
Butter or margarine	2 tbsp.	30 mL
Salt	1 tsp.	5 mL
Pepper	¼ tsp.	1 mL
Tomatoes, peeled, seeded and cut up	5	5
Basil	1 tsp.	5 mL
Grated Parmesan cheese		

(continued on next page)

In large uncovered saucepan cook fettuccine in boiling water, cooking oil and first amount of salt until tender but firm, about 9 to 11 minutes. Drain.

Sauté next 6 ingredients in frying pan until soft, about 7 minutes.

Dip tomatoes in boiling water for about 1 minute, until they will peel easily. Add cut up tomatoes and basil. Sauté for 2 to 3 minutes more. Stir in fettuccine. Turn into serving bowl.

Sprinkle with Parmesan cheese or serve cheese separately. Makes 6 cups (1.5 L).

Variation: Stir in 1 tsp. (5 mL) chili powder. Good.

PASTA WITH BEAN SAUCE

Serve with a salad and dinner roll and you've got a meal. Very good.

Elbow macaroni	2 cups	500 mL
Boiling water	2½ qts.	3 L
Cooking oil (optional)	1 tbsp.	15 mL
Salt	2 tsp.	10 mL
Chopped onion	1 cup	250 mL
Chopped green pepper	¼ cup	60 mL
Butter or margarine	2 tbsp.	30 mL
Kidney beans, drained	14 oz.	398 mL
Canned tomatoes, broken up	14 oz.	398 mL
Tomato sauce	7½ oz.	213 mL
Basil	½ tsp.	2 mL
Marjoram	½ tsp.	2 mL
Oregano	½ tsp.	2 mL
Salt	½ tsp.	2 mL
Grated medium Cheddar cheese	1 cup	250 mL

Cook macaroni in boiling water, cooking oil and first amount of salt in uncovered large saucepan until tender but firm, about 5 to 7 minutes. Drain. Return macaroni to pot.

While macaroni cooks, sauté onion and green pepper in butter in large saucepan until soft.

Add remaining ingredients. Heat stirring often until hot and cheese is melted. Stir into macaroni. Makes about 10 cups (2.2 L).

MACARONI AND CHEESE DELUXE

It is difficult to decide which ranks highest, flavor or color.

Elbow macaroni	2 cups	500 mL
Boiling water	2½ qts.	3 L
Cooking oil (optional)	1 tbsp.	15 mL
Salt	2 tsp.	10 mL
Grated sharp or medium Cheddar cheese	4 cups	1 L
Condensed cream of mushroom soup	10 oz.	284 mL
Sliced mushrooms, drained	10 oz.	284 mL
Finely chopped onion	1 cup	250 mL
Mayonnaise	¾ cup	175 mL
Finely chopped green pepper (optional but flavorful)	¼ cup	60 mL
Chopped pimiento	2 tbsp.	30 mL

In large uncovered saucepan cook macaroni in boiling water, cooking oil and salt until tender but firm, about 5 to 7 minutes. Drain. Return macaroni to pot.

Add remaining ingredients. Mix. Pour into 2½ quart (3 L) greased casserole. Bake uncovered in 350°F (180°C) oven for 30 to 40 minutes. Serves 8.

Pictured on page 125.

BROCCOLI PASTA

Very colorful with a choice of a creamy variation.

Medium egg noodles	8 oz.	250 g
Boiling water	2½ qts.	3 L
Cooking oil (optional)	1 tbsp.	15 mL
Salt	2 tsp.	10 mL
Olive oil (or cooking oil)	¼ cup	60 mL
Garlic cloves, minced	4	4
Fresh broccoli, coarsely chopped	4 cups	1 L
Chopped walnuts	½ cup	125 mL
Salt, sprinkle		
Pepper, sprinkle		
Pitted black olives, sliced (optional)	⅓ cup	75 mL
Grated Parmesan cheese, heavy sprinkle		

(continued on next page)

In large uncovered saucepan cook noodles in boiling water, cooking oil and first amount of salt until tender but firm, about 5 to 7 minutes. Drain. Return noodles to pot. Keep warm.

Meanwhile put olive oil into frying pan or wok. Add garlic cloves. Sauté until golden, about 2 to 3 minutes.

Add broccoli and stir-fry until tender-crisp.

Add nuts, second amount of salt, pepper and olives. Mix. Heat through. Turn pasta out onto warm platter. Spoon vegetable mixture over top.

Sprinkle with cheese. Serves 3 to 4.

Variation: Add ½ cup (125 mL) whipping cream and ¼ cup (60 mL) grated Parmesan cheese to the drained pasta. Heat, then add rest of ingredients.

SHADES OF PASTA

This mushroom and onion pasta contains the colorful vegetable noodles.

Vegetable noodles	8 oz.	250 g
Boiling water	2½ qts.	3 L
Cooking oil (optional)	1 tbsp.	15 mL
Salt	2 tsp.	10 mL
Butter or margarine	2 tbsp.	30 mL
Sliced fresh mushrooms	4 cups	1 L
Thinly sliced onion	1½ cups	375 mL
Whipping cream	1 cup	250 mL
Grated Parmesan cheese	2 tbsp.	30 mL
Salt	1 tsp.	5 mL
Dill weed (or use ½ as much nutmeg)	½ tsp.	2 mL
Grated Parmesan cheese		

Cook noodles in boiling water, cooking oil and first amount of salt until tender but firm, about 6 to 8 minutes. Drain. Return noodles to pot.

Meanwhile melt butter in frying pan. Add mushrooms and onion. Sauté until soft. This may need to be done in two batches. Add more butter if needed.

Add cream, first amount of Parmesan cheese, second amount of salt and dill weed. Heat. Add to noodles. Toss together. Transfer to warm platter.

Sprinkle with remaining Parmesan cheese. Serves 4.

PASTA PRIMAVERA

A grand dish. Great any time of year with an abundance of fresh vegetables readily available.

Coarsely chopped broccoli (or use same amount fresh asparagus)	2 cups	500 mL
Zucchini, cut in fingers, about 1 medium	2 cups	500 mL
Frozen snow peas, or fresh	6 oz.	170 g
Frozen peas, or fresh	1 cup	250 mL
Boiling salted water		
Cherry tomatoes, halved, or large tomato chopped in coarse chunks	12	12
Fresh chopped parsley	¼ cup	60 mL
Garlic clove, minced (or ¼ tsp., 1 mL, garlic powder)	1	1
Olive oil (or cooking oil)	1 tbsp.	15 mL
Olive oil (or cooking oil)	2 tbsp.	30 mL
Garlic clove, minced (or ¼ tsp., 1 mL, garlic powder)	1	1
Sliced fresh mushrooms	2 cups	500 mL
Spaghetti or linguini	1 lb.	500 g
Boiling water	4 qts.	5 L
Cooking oil (optional)	1 tbsp.	15 mL
Salt	1 tbsp.	15 mL
Whipping cream	1 cup	250 mL
Grated Parmesan cheese	½ cup	125 mL
Salt, good sprinkle		
Pepper, sprinkle		
Dried basil	2 tsp.	10 mL
Grated Parmesan cheese, sprinkle (fresh is best)		

Cook broccoli, zucchini, snow peas and peas in boiling salted water for 3 minutes until tender-crisp. Drain. This may be prepared well ahead of time.

In another pan sauté tomatoes, parsley and first garlic clove in first amount of olive oil for about 5 minutes.

In large frying pan or wok heat second amount of olive oil. Sauté second garlic clove and mushrooms until soft. Add broccoli, zucchini, snow peas, peas and tomato mixture. Heat through. Stir often.

(continued on next page)

Cook spaghetti in boiling water, cooking oil and first amount of salt in uncovered Dutch oven until tender but firm, about 11 to 13 minutes. Drain.

Combine pasta with mushroom-vegetable mixture. Add cream, first amount of Parmesan cheese, second amount of salt, pepper and basil. Toss together. Add tomato mixture. Toss lightly. Put into serving bowl.

Sprinkle with Parmesan cheese. Serves 4.

Pictured on cover.

CHILI BEAN PASTA

Protein galore! And so very good. Add more chili powder if you like.

Butter or margarine	2 tbsp.	30 mL
Chopped onion	1¼ cups	300 mL
Chopped green pepper	⅓ cup	75 mL
Canned tomatoes, mashed	14 oz.	398 mL
Kidney beans, drained	14 oz.	398 mL
Tomato sauce	7½ oz.	213 mL
Grated Cheddar cheese	2 cups	500 mL
Chili powder	2 tsp.	10 mL
Worcestershire sauce	1 tsp.	5 mL
Salt	½ tsp.	2 mL
Elbow macaroni	2 cups	500 mL
Boiling water	2½ qts.	3 L
Cooking oil (optional)	1 tbsp.	15 mL
Salt	2 tsp.	10 mL

Melt butter in large saucepan. Add onion and green pepper. Sauté until soft.

Add next 7 ingredients. Heat and stir until mixture simmers.

In separate large uncovered saucepan cook macaroni in boiling water, cooking oil and second amount of salt until tender but firm, about 5 to 7 minutes. Drain. Mix macaroni with sauce and serve. Makes about 10 cups (2.2 L).

BROWNED BUTTER NOODLES

So good and with so few ingredients. Try this with and without poppy seeds.

Fettuccine	8 oz.	250 g
Boiling water	2½ qts.	3 L
Cooking oil (optional)	1 tbsp.	15 mL
Salt	2 tsp.	10 mL
Butter or margarine	¼ cup	60 mL
Salt	½ tsp.	2 mL
Poppy seeds (optional)	1 tbsp.	15 mL

In large uncovered saucepan cook noodles in boiling water, cooking oil and first amount of salt until tender but firm, about 5 to 7 minutes. Drain. Return fettuccine to pot.

Put butter and second amount of salt into saucepan over medium heat. Allow butter to brown being careful not to scorch. If you are adding poppy seeds, add them to the butter and salt before browning. Add to fettuccine. Toss. Serve in bowl. Makes 4 cups (1 L).

1. Tortellini page 117
2. Bowl Of Bows page 25
3. Apricot Noodle Pudding page 145
4. Spinach Stuffed Manicotti page 112

FETTUCCINE WITH HAM

A good one pot dish flavored just right with parsley and thyme.

Fettuccine	1 lb.	500 g
Boiling water	4 qts.	5 L
Cooking oil (optional)	1 tbsp.	15 mL
Salt	1 tbsp.	15 mL
Butter or margarine, melted	¼ cup	60 mL
Salt	1 tsp.	5 mL
Pepper	⅛ tsp.	0.5 mL
Chopped ham, or flakes or strips	1 cup	250 mL
Grated Parmesan cheese	½ cup	125 mL
Parsley flakes (or use 3 to 4 times more of fresh, chopped)	4 tsp.	20 mL
Thyme	¼ tsp.	1 mL

Cook fettuccine in boiling water, cooking oil and first amount of salt until tender but firm, about 5 to 7 minutes. Drain. Return noodles to pot.

Add butter, second amount of salt and pepper. Toss.

Add remaining 4 ingredients. Heat and toss until hot and flavors are mixed. Makes about 8 cups (2 L).

WIENER AND PASTA POT

What could be easier than combining raw pasta with everything else and simmering until done? Economical.

Condensed tomato soup	2 × 10 oz.	2 × 284 mL
Water	2 cups	500 mL
Sliced mushrooms, with juice	10 oz.	284 mL
Wieners, cut bite size	1 lb.	454 g
Tiny pasta shells	8 oz.	225 g
Chili powder	2 tsp.	10 mL

In large saucepan or Dutch oven combine all 6 ingredients. Cover. Cook slowly until shells are tender but firm, about 15 to 17 minutes. Makes 8 cups (1.8 L).

Pictured on page 107.

CAULIFLOWER CHEESE PASTA

Made of large shells in a cheese sauce and browned crumb topping. Tastes as good as it looks.

Large pasta shells (not jumbo)	4 oz.	125 g
Boiling water	2½ qts.	3 L
Cooking oil (optional)	1 tbsp.	15 mL
Salt	2 tsp.	10 mL
Butter or margarine	3 tbsp.	50 mL
All-purpose flour	3 tbsp.	50 mL
Salt	1 tsp.	5 mL
Pepper	⅛ tsp.	0.5 mL
Milk	1½ cups	350 mL
Grated medium Cheddar cheese	1 cup	250 mL
Coarsely chopped cauliflower	2 cups	500 mL
Salted water		
Dry bread crumbs	½ cup	125 mL
Butter or margarine, melted	2 tbsp.	30 mL

Cook shells in boiling water, cooking oil and first amount of salt in large uncovered saucepan until tender but firm, about 13 to 16 minutes.

Meanwhile melt butter in saucepan. Mix in flour, second amount of salt and pepper. Stir in milk until it boils and thickens. Stir in cheese.

Cook cauliflower in salted water until tender-crisp. Drain. Add to sauce. Drain shells and add. Mix together. Put into greased 2 quart (2 L) casserole.

Mix bread crumbs with melted butter. Spread over top. Bake uncovered in 350ºF (180ºC) oven for about 25 minutes until browned and hot. Serves 4.

Paré Pointer

If you want to lose weight — walk pasta bakery, pasta desserts, pasta candy store and have someone pasta rabbit food.

It is better to cook the "straw and hay" separately according to package directions since cooking times often vary. This has a head start on a meal. Good pasta. Praw-SHOO-toe ham is used although cooked ham may be substituted.

Butter or margarine	¼ cup	60 mL
Garlic clove, quartered	1	1
Fresh mushrooms, sliced	1 lb.	500 g
Proscuitto ham, cut in matchsticks (or use cooked ham)	½ lb.	225 g
Whipping cream	¾ cup	175 mL
Salt	½ tsp.	2 mL
Pepper	¼ tsp.	1 mL
Green fettuccine	8 oz.	250 g
White fettuccine	8 oz.	250 g
Grated Parmesan cheese	½ cup	125 mL
Grated Parmesan cheese, sprinkle		

Melt butter in frying pan. Sauté garlic until browned. Remove garlic with slotted spoon and discard.

Add mushrooms in 1 or 2 bunches. Sauté until soft. Sauté ham until browned adding more butter if needed. Transfer to large saucepan to keep warm.

Stir cream, salt and pepper into frying pan loosening all bits from bottom. Pour over mushrooms. Keep warm.

Cook green and white fettuccine according to package directions until tender but firm. Drain. Add to mushroom mixture with first amount of Parmesan cheese. Toss together. Turn out onto serving platter or into bowl. Sprinkle with remaining Parmesan cheese. Serves 8.

Pictured on page 107.

Pare Pointer

They keep their hens in the basement. They are laying in a supply of coal.

CHICKEN FETTUCCINE

It is amazing how green noodles fade into a most pleasing color for eating. Delicious.

Green fettuccine	8 oz.	250 g
Boiling water	2½ qts.	3 L
Cooking oil (optional)	1 tbsp.	15 mL
Salt	2 tsp.	10 mL
Cooked chicken or turkey, cubed	4 cups	1 L
Condensed cream of chicken soup	10 oz.	284 mL
Sour cream	1 cup	250 mL
Chopped green onion	¼ cup	60 mL
White wine (or apple juice)	3 tbsp.	50 mL
Salt	1 tsp.	5 mL
Grated medium Cheddar cheese	1 cup	250 mL

Cook fettuccine in boiling water, cooking oil and first amount of salt in uncovered Dutch oven until tender but firm, about 9 to 11 minutes. Drain. Put fettuccine into greased 3 quart (3.5 L) casserole.

Spread chicken over fettuccine.

Mix soup with sour cream, onion, wine and second amount of salt in bowl. Spoon mixture over chicken.

Spread cheese over all. Cover. Bake in 350°F (180°C) oven for 30 minutes. Bake about another 10 minutes uncovered to brown a bit. Serves 6 to 8.

HAM FETTUCCINE

This creamy dish has a mild dill flavor. Contains slivered ham. Feel free to add more ham for extra hungry folks.

Fettuccine	8 oz.	250 g
Boiling water	2½ qts.	3 L
Cooking oil (optional)	1 tbsp.	15 mL
Salt	2 tsp.	10 mL
Whipping cream	1 cup	250 mL
Dill weed	½ tsp.	2 mL
Cooked ham slices, slivered (about 4 slices)	½ cup	125 mL
Salt	½ tsp.	2 mL
Pepper, light sprinkle		
Grated Parmesan cheese (optional)		

(continued on next page)

Cook fettuccine in boiling water, cooking oil and first amount of salt in large uncovered saucepan until tender but firm, about 5 to 7 minutes.

While pasta is cooking bring cream and dill weed to a boil in medium saucepan. Add ham, second amount of salt and pepper. Bring to a boil again. Drain pasta. Add to creamy-ham mixture. Toss and serve.

Parmesan cheese may be sprinkled over top but go easy as it tends to cover the dill flavor. Makes 5⅓ cups (1.2 L).

CORNED PASTA

This colorful dish is easy to prepare. Pasta is added raw. Kernel corn adds to both taste and color.

Olive oil (or cooking oil)	1 tbsp.	15 mL
Lean ground beef	1 lb.	500 g
Chopped onion	2 cups	500 mL
Small green pepper, chopped	1	1
Canned tomatoes, mashed	28 oz.	796 mL
Kernel corn, drained	12 oz.	341 mL
Water	¾ cup	175 mL
Pasta wagon wheels, uncooked	8 oz.	250 g
Salt	1 tsp.	5 mL
Pepper	¼ tsp.	1 mL
Garlic powder	¼ tsp.	1 mL
Sliced black olives (optional)	¼ cup	60 mL
Grated medium Cheddar cheese	1 cup	250 mL

Heat olive oil in large saucepan. Add ground beef, onion and green pepper. Scramble-fry until browned.

Add next 8 ingredients to meat mixture. Mix together. Cover. Simmer gently until pasta is tender but firm, about 8 minutes. Stir occasionally.

Stir in cheese and serve. Makes 8 cups (2 L).

Variation: If you prefer, turn into 3 quart (3.5 L) greased casserole before adding cheese. Sprinkle cheese over top. Bake uncovered in 350°F (180°C) oven until cheese melts, about 10 to 15 minutes.

Pictured on page 107.

SPAGHETTI AND MEATBALLS

Everyone knows this pasta dish. Meatballs are cooked in the sauce.

MEATBALLS

Lean ground beef	1 lb.	500 g
Chopped onion	½ cup	125 mL
Dry bread crumbs	½ cup	125 mL
Grated Parmesan cheese	¼ cup	60 mL
Salt	1 tsp.	5 mL
Pepper	¼ tsp.	1 mL
Eggs	2	2

Combine all 7 ingredients in medium size bowl. Mix well. Shape into about 28 meatballs. Set aside.

SPAGHETTI SAUCE

Chopped onion	1 cup	250 mL
Canned tomatoes, mashed	28 oz.	796 mL
Tomato paste	5½ oz.	156 mL
Sliced mushrooms, drained	10 oz.	284 mL
Granulated sugar	2 tsp.	10 mL
Parsley flakes	1 tsp.	5 mL
Salt	1 tsp.	5 mL
Pepper	¼ tsp.	1 mL
Bay leaf	1	1

Measure all 9 ingredients into large saucepan. Mix. Stir occasionally as sauce simmers uncovered for 20 minutes. Add meatballs. Cover and simmer 20 to 25 minutes more. Discard bay leaf.

SPAGHETTI

Spaghetti	8 oz.	250 g
Boiling water	2½ qts.	3 L
Cooking oil (optional)	1 tbsp.	15 mL
Salt	2 tsp.	10 mL
Grated Parmesan cheese	½ cup	125 mL

Cook spaghetti in boiling water, cooking oil and salt in uncovered Dutch oven until tender but firm, about 11 to 13 minutes. Drain. Arrange on warm platter or 4 plates. Spoon meatballs and sauce over center of spaghetti.

Sprinkle heavily with Parmesan cheese. Serves 4.

Pictured on page 53.

Steak strips marinated in a ginger and soy sauce add to these noodles. Good.

MARINADE

Soy sauce	⅓ cup	75 mL
Cornstarch	2 tsp.	10 mL
Cider vinegar	2 tsp.	10 mL
Granulated sugar	1 tsp.	5 mL
Ginger	½ tsp.	2 mL
Salt	½ tsp.	2 mL
Sirloin steak	2 lbs.	1 kg
Peanut oil (or cooking oil)	¼ cup	60 mL
Garlic cloves, minced	2	2
Medium carrots, cut in matchsticks	3 - 4	3 - 4
Celery ribs, cut in matchsticks	2 - 3	2 - 3
Water	⅔ cup	150 mL
Soy sauce	2 tbsp.	30 mL
Chicken bouillon powder	1 tsp.	5 mL
Cornstarch	1 tbsp.	15 mL
Medium egg noodles	12 oz.	375 g
Boiling water	3 qts.	4 L
Cooking oil (optional)	1 tbsp.	15 mL
Salt	1 tbsp.	15 mL

Marinade: Mix first 6 ingredients together. Put into plastic bag.

Slice steak into ¼ × 3 inch (6 × 75 mm) long strips. This is easier to do if meat is partially frozen. Put into marinade in bag for 20 minutes.

Heat peanut oil in frying pan. Add garlic. Add meat and any remaining marinade. Sauté meat to brown, about 5 to 8 minutes. Remove meat to dish.

Add carrots and celery to pan. Sauté until tender-crisp, about 5 minutes.

Measure water in cup. Add soy sauce, bouillon powder and cornstarch. Mix. Pour into vegetables. Add meat. Stir to boil and thicken. Keep hot.

In large saucepan, cook noodles, uncovered, in boiling water, cooking oil and second amount of salt until tender but firm, about 5 to 7 minutes. Drain. Put noodles back into pot. Add meat mixture and toss. Noodles will turn dark. If you prefer white noodles, spoon meat mixture over center of noodles on platter or individual plates. Serves 4.

SAUSAGE ZUCCHINI FRY

Bits of carrot, green onion and mushrooms make this a colorful dish.
Sausage flavor is mild. Mild Italian sausage is also very good to use.

Sausage meat	1 lb.	500 g
Zucchini with peel, quartered and sliced	4 cups	1 L
Sliced fresh mushrooms	1 cup	250 mL
Grated carrot	1 cup	250 mL
Sliced green onions	¼ cup	60 mL
Seasoned salt	1½ tsp.	7 mL
Pepper	¼ tsp.	1 mL
Spaghetti	1 lb.	500 g
Boiling water	4 qts.	5 L
Cooking oil (optional)	1 tbsp.	15 mL
Salt	1 tbsp.	15 mL
Grated Parmesan cheese		

Put sausage meat into frying pan. Scramble-fry until no pink color remains in meat.

Add next 6 ingredients to meat. Sauté for about 15 minutes. Stir occasionally.

Meanwhile, in uncovered Dutch oven cook spaghetti in boiling water, cooking oil and salt until tender but firm, about 11 to 13 minutes. Drain. Combine with meat mixture. Toss together. Transfer to bowl or platter.

Sprinkle with Parmesan cheese. Makes about 9⅓ cups (2.3 L).

PIQUANT PASTA

A bit of vinegar zips this up along with some barbecue sauce and chili.

Olive oil (or cooking oil)	2 tbsp.	30 mL
Lean ground beef	1½ lbs.	750 g
Chopped onion	1½ cups	375 mL
Condensed cream of onion soup	10 oz.	284 mL
Condensed tomato soup	10 oz.	284 mL
Vinegar	¼ cup	60 mL
Barbecue sauce	3 tbsp.	50 mL
Chili powder	1 tsp.	5 mL
Salt	1 tsp.	5 mL
Pepper	¼ tsp.	1 mL

(continued on next page)

Egg noodles, medium or broad	1 lb.	500 g
Boiling water	4 qts.	5 L
Cooking oil (optional)	1 tbsp.	15 mL
Salt	1 tbsp.	15 mL

Heat olive oil in frying pan. Add ground beef and chopped onion. Scramble-fry until browned.

Stir in both soups, vinegar, barbecue sauce, chili powder, first amount of salt and pepper. Simmer gently to blend flavors. Stir occasionally.

Cook noodles in boiling water, cooking oil and second amount of salt in uncovered Dutch oven until tender but firm, about 5 to 7 minutes. Drain. Add to meat mixture. Stir together. Makes 8 generous cups (2 L).

GROUND BEEF AND NOODLES

This tasty dish gives two options. Either mix everything together or serve pasta on plates with sauce spooned over top.

Lean ground beef	1½ lbs.	750 g
Chopped onion	1½ cups	375 mL
Cooking oil	1½ tbsp.	25 mL
Condensed tomato soup	10 oz.	284 mL
Condensed cream of mushroom soup	10 oz.	284 mL
Salt	1 tsp.	5 mL
Pepper	¼ tsp.	1 mL
Egg noodles, medium or broad	1 lb.	500 g
Boiling water	4 qts.	5 L
Cooking oil (optional)	1 tbsp.	15 mL
Salt	1 tbsp.	15 mL

In frying pan scramble-fry ground beef and onion in first amount of cooking oil until browned.

Add next 4 ingredients. Mix. Heat through.

Cook noodles in boiling water, remaining cooking oil and second amount of salt in uncovered Dutch oven until tender but firm, about 5 to 7 minutes. Drain. Return noodles to pot. Add meat sauce. Mix all together. Makes about 8 cups (2 L).

BEEFY BACON PASTA

No pre-cooking of pasta. This has a bacon and chili flavor. More chili powder may be added if desired.

Bacon slices	4	4
Lean ground beef	1 lb.	500 g
Chopped onion	½ cup	125 mL
Water	3 cups	750 mL
Tomato paste	5½ oz.	156 mL
Elbow macaroni, uncooked	1½ cups	375 mL
Chili powder	1½ tsp.	7 mL
Granulated sugar	1 tsp.	5 mL
Salt	2 tsp.	10 mL
Pepper	¼ tsp.	1 mL
Parsley flakes	1 tsp.	5 mL
Garlic powder	¼ tsp.	1 mL

Fry bacon in large saucepan. Remove bacon to plate. Cut into small pieces. Set aside.

Put beef and onion into same saucepan. Scramble-fry until browned. Drain and discard excess fat.

Add remaining ingredients to beef and onion in saucepan. Add bacon. Stir. Cover and simmer slowly until macaroni is cooked, about 10 to 15 minutes. Makes about 6 cups (1.5 L).

PASTA WITH ADOBO SAUCE

Pasta with a superb topping of pork cooked in spices. Chicken may be interchanged with pork if desired.

Pork, cut in small cubes	1 lb.	500 g
Chopped onion	¼ cup	60 mL
Vinegar	⅓ cup	75 mL
Soy sauce	4 tsp.	25 mL
Salt	¾ tsp.	4 mL
Pepper	⅛ tsp.	0.5 mL
Garlic powder (or 1 clove, minced)	¼ tsp.	1 mL
Water	½ cup	125 mL
Small bay leaf	1	1
Juice, plus water to make	1 cup	250 mL
Cornstarch	1 tbsp.	15 mL

(continued on next page)

Linguini	8 oz.	250 g
Boiling water	2½ qts.	3 L
Cooking oil (optional)	1 tbsp.	15 mL
Salt	2 tsp.	10 mL

Combine first 9 ingredients in saucepan. Bring to a boil. Cover. Simmer slowly until meat is tender, about 30 minutes. Discard bay leaf.

Drain juice left on meat into measuring cup. Add water to make 1 cup (250 mL). Mix cornstarch into cool water and juice mixture. Add to meat. Stir and heat to boil and thicken.

Cook linguini in boiling water, cooking oil and second amount of salt in uncovered Dutch oven, until tender but firm, about 11 to 13 minutes. Drain. Arrange on 4 warmed plates. Spoon meat sauce over top. Makes about 2⅔ cups (600 mL) sauce. Serves 4.

ALL-IN-ONE MACARONI

Talk about easy! The pasta is added raw.

Lean ground beef	1 lb.	500 g
Chopped onion	½ cup	125 mL
Garlic clove, minced	1	1
Cooking oil	1 tbsp.	15 mL
Tomatoes, mashed	14 oz.	398 mL
Water	1½ cups	350 mL
Soy sauce	1 tbsp.	15 mL
Basil	⅛ tsp.	0.5 mL
Thyme	⅛ tsp.	0.5 mL
Elbow macaroni	2 cups	500 mL
Salt	1 tsp.	5 mL
Pepper	⅛ tsp.	0.5 mL
Granulated sugar	½ tsp.	2 mL

In Dutch oven or large saucepan brown meat, onion and garlic in cooking oil.

Add remaining 9 ingredients. Bring to a boil. Cover and simmer, stirring occasionally until macaroni is tender but firm, about 15 minutes. Serves 4.

SPAGHETTI AND MEAT SAUCE

Creamy white noodles covered with a thick dark sauce and topped with Parmesan cheese.

Spaghetti	8 oz.	250 g
Boiling water	2½ qts.	3 L
Cooking oil (optional)	1 tbsp.	15 mL
Salt	2 tsp.	10 mL
SPAGHETTI MEAT SAUCE		
Lean ground beef	1½ lbs.	750 g
Finely chopped onion	½ cup	125 mL
Cooking oil	1 tbsp.	15 mL
Tomato sauce	7½ oz.	213 mL
Tomato paste	5½ oz.	156 mL
Sliced mushrooms, with juice	10 oz.	284 mL
Envelope dry onion soup	1	1
Parsley flakes	2 tsp.	10 mL

Grated Parmesan cheese, sprinkle

Cook spaghetti in boiling water, cooking oil and salt in uncovered Dutch oven until tender but firm, about 11 to 13 minutes.

Spaghetti Meat Sauce: Meanwhile, scramble-fry ground beef and onion in cooking oil in frying pan until browned.

Combine tomato sauce, tomato paste, mushrooms with juice, onion soup and parsley flakes in large saucepan. Add meat mixture. Cover. Simmer 5 minutes. Stir occasionally. This makes about 4½ cups (1 L) sauce.

Drain spaghetti and divide among 4 warm plates. Spoon meat sauce over top. Sprinkle with Parmesan cheese. Serves 4.

Pare Pointer

To err is human. To put the blame on someone else is even more human.

Good stuff!

Olive oil (or cooking oil)	1 tbsp.	15 mL
Lean ground beef	1 lb.	500 g
Chopped onion	1 cup	250 mL
Chopped celery	¾ cup	175 mL
Spaghetti	8 oz.	250 g
Boiling water	2½ qts.	3 L
Cooking oil (optional)	1 tbsp.	15 mL
Salt	2 tsp.	10 mL
Canned tomatoes, mashed	28 oz.	796 mL
Sliced mushrooms, drained	10 oz.	284 mL
Granulated sugar	1 tbsp.	15 mL
Salt	2 tsp.	10 mL
Pepper	¼ tsp.	1 mL

Heat olive oil in frying pan. Add ground beef, onion and celery. Scramble-fry until browned, about 7 to 8 minutes.

In large uncovered saucepan or Dutch oven cook spaghetti in boiling water, cooking oil and first amount of salt until tender but firm, about 11 to 13 minutes. Drain. Return spaghetti to pot. Add meat mixture.

Add remaining ingredients. Cover. Simmer slowly for about 10 to 15 minutes. Stir occasionally. Add a bit of water if it gets too dry. Taste for salt and pepper. If you want more color add 14 oz. (398 mL) drained cut green beans. Makes 8 cups (1.9 L).

Paré Pointer

Someone who gets his head stuck in a bucket is better known as a pail face.

FETTUCCINE WITH TOMATO

What better combination than bacon and tomato.

Bacon slices, diced	8	8
Chopped onion	1½ cups	375 mL
Tomatoes, peeled, seeded and cubed	4	4
Chopped fresh parsley	¼ cup	60 mL
Basil	1 tsp.	5 mL
Garlic powder	½ tsp.	2 mL
Fettuccine	1 lb.	500 g
Boiling water	4 qts.	5 L
Cooking oil (optional)	1 tbsp.	15 mL
Salt	1 tbsp.	15 mL
Butter or margarine, melted	¼ cup	60 mL
Salt	1 tsp.	5 mL
Pepper	⅛ tsp.	0.5 mL
Grated Parmesan cheese		

Sauté bacon pieces and onion in frying pan until onion is soft and clear.

Add tomatoes, parsley, basil and garlic powder. Stir and heat through. Keep warm.

In uncovered Dutch oven cook fettuccine in boiling water, cooking oil and first amount of salt until tender but firm, about 5 to 7 minutes. Drain. Return to pot.

Add butter, second amount of salt and pepper to fettuccine. Toss. Add tomato mixture. Toss. Taste for salt and pepper, adding some if needed.

Sprinkle with or pass Parmesan cheese on the side. Makes about 8 cups (2 L).

Note: To peel tomatoes, immerse in boiling water for about one minute or until skins will peel easily.

Paré Pointer

No wonder a computer can do so much work so fast. It doesn't have to answer the phone.

Add a green salad and you have a great meal.

Lean ground beef	1½ lbs.	750 g
Chopped onion	1 cup	250 mL
Cooking oil	2 tbsp.	30 mL
Condensed cream of mushroom soup	10 oz.	284 mL
Sauerkraut, drained	14 oz.	398 mL
Salt	1 tsp.	5 mL
Pepper	¼ tsp.	1 mL
Wide egg noodles	8 oz.	250 g
Boiling water	2½ qts.	3 L
Cooking oil (optional)	1 tbsp.	15 mL
Salt	2 tsp.	10 mL
Dry bread crumbs	¼ cup	60 mL
Grated Parmesan cheese	¼ cup	60 mL
Butter or margarine, melted	1 tbsp.	15 mL

Brown meat and onion in first amount of cooking oil in large saucepan. Break up meat well.

Add soup, sauerkraut, first amount of salt and pepper to meat and onion.

Cook noodles in boiling water, remaining cooking oil and second amount of salt until tender but firm, about 5 to 7 minutes. Drain. Combine with meat mixture. This may be served as is, or put into 3 quart (3 L) greased casserole.

Mix bread crumbs, cheese and butter together. Sprinkle over top. Bake uncovered in 350°F (180°C) oven until browned and heated through, about 30 minutes. Serves 6.

Paré Pointer

Billy's dad had Abraham Lincoln's watch but Johnny's dad had Adam's apple.

SPAGHETTI TWO STEP

A simple meaty dish. Can easily be stretched with the addition of a bit more pasta. Good flavor.

Lean ground beef	1 lb.	500 g
Chopped onion	1½ cups	375 mL
Cooking oil	1 tbsp.	15 mL
Condensed tomato soup	10 oz.	284 mL
Salt	1 tsp.	5 mL
Pepper	⅛ tsp.	0.5 mL
Spaghetti	8 oz.	250 g
Boiling water	2½ qts.	3 L
Cooking oil (optional)	1 tbsp.	15 mL
Salt	2 tsp.	10 mL

Scramble-fry beef and onion in first amount of cooking oil until no pink in meat remains and onion is soft. Drain and discard any excess fat.

Add soup, first amount of salt and pepper. Stir and heat through.

Cook spaghetti in boiling water, second amounts of cooking oil and salt in uncovered Dutch oven until tender but firm, about 11 to 13 minutes. Drain. Add to meat mixture. Stir together. Taste for salt and pepper, adding more if needed. Makes 6 cups (1.5 L).

1. Pot Stickers with Hotshot Sauce page 118
2. Singapore Noodles page 98
3. Far East Tuna Salad page 30
4. Teriyaki Chicken Salad page 22

SPAGHETTI CHEESE BAKE

This outstanding spaghetti casserole is superior. Make this one of your first-to-try recipes.

Spaghetti	8 oz.	250 g
Boiling water	2½ qts.	3 L
Cooking oil (optional)	1 tbsp.	15 mL
Salt	2 tsp.	10 mL
Cooking oil	1 tbsp.	15 mL
Lean ground beef	1 lb.	500 g
Chopped onion	1 cup	250 mL
Condensed cream of mushroom soup	10 oz.	284 mL
Condensed tomato soup	10 oz.	284 mL
Water	½ cup	125 mL
Seasoned salt	1 tsp.	5 mL
Pepper	¼ tsp.	1 mL
Grated medium Cheddar cheese	2 cups	500 mL
Dry bread crumbs	½ cup	125 mL
Butter or margarine, melted	2 tbsp.	30 mL
Grated medium Cheddar cheese	¼ cup	60 mL

In large uncovered saucepan cook spaghetti in boiling water, first amounts of cooking oil and salt until tender but firm, about 11 to 13 minutes. Drain. Return spaghetti to pot.

Heat second amount of cooking oil in frying pan. Add beef and onion. Scramble-fry until no pink remains and onion is soft.

Add mushroom soup, tomato soup, water, seasoned salt and pepper to meat mixture. Simmer slowly, uncovered for 10 to 15 minutes.

Add first amount of cheese. Stir to melt. Mix with spaghetti. Turn into 2½ to 3 quart (3 to 3.5 L) greased casserole.

Mix bread crumbs with melted butter in small saucepan. Stir in remaining cheese. Sprinkle over top. Bake uncovered in 350°F (180°C) oven for about 20 to 30 minutes or until hot and browned. Serves 6 to 8.

Fare Pointer

When angels get colds they use miracle drugs.

MUSHROOM NOODLES

A light creamy sauce envelopes these mushrooms and noodles. Good.

Egg noodles, medium or broad	8 oz.	250 g
Boiling water	2½ qts.	3 L
Cooking oil (optional)	1 tbsp.	15 mL
Salt	2 tsp.	10 mL
Butter or margarine	2 tbsp.	30 mL
Sliced fresh mushrooms	4 cups	1 L
Chopped onion	½ cup	125 mL
Butter or margarine	1 tbsp	15 mL
All-purpose flour	1 tbsp.	15 mL
Seasoned salt	1 tsp.	5 mL
Milk	⅔ cup	150 mL
White wine (or apple juice)	¼ cup	60 mL
Grated mozzarella cheese	1 cup	250 mL
Grated mozzarella cheese	1 cup	250 mL

In large uncovered saucepan cook noodles in boiling water, cooking oil and salt until tender but firm, about 5 to 7 minutes. Drain. Return noodles to pot.

Melt first amount of butter in frying pan. Add mushrooms and onion. Sauté until soft. Add to noodles. Keep hot.

Melt second amount of butter in small saucepan. Mix in flour and seasoned salt. Stir in milk until it boils and thickens. Add wine. Add to noodles.

Add first amount of mozzarella cheese to noodles. Toss all together well.

This may be served now on a warm platter with remaining cheese sprinkled over top or it can be put into a 2 quart (2 L) casserole, sprinkled with remaining cheese and heated in 350°F (180°C) oven long enough to melt cheese, about 10 minutes. Makes 4 cups (1 L).

Paré Pointer

It is doubtful that any machine can clear the driveway of snow faster than a teenager who needs the car for a date.

A different type of chili. A large recipe that makes a good take-along dish. Easy to make half as much.

Cooking oil	2 tbsp.	30 mL
Chopped onion	3 cups	750 mL
Lean ground beef	2 lbs.	1 kg
Green pepper, chopped	1	1
Tomatoes, mashed	28 oz.	796 mL
Condensed tomato soup	10 oz.	284 mL
Tomato paste	2 x 5½ oz.	2 x 156 mL
Worcestershire sauce	4 tbsp.	60 mL
Granulated sugar	2 tbsp.	30 mL
Chili powder	2 tsp.	10 mL
Salt	2 tsp.	10 mL
Pepper	¼ tsp.	1 mL
Spaghetti	1 lb.	500 g
Boiling water	4 qts.	5 L
Cooking oil (optional)	1 tbsp.	15 mL
Salt	1 tbsp.	15 mL
Grated medium Cheddar cheese	2 cups	500 mL

Scramble-fry first 4 ingredients in batches until browned.

Put next 8 ingredients into large pot. Add meat mixture. Simmer for 5 minutes.

In uncovered Dutch oven cook spaghetti in boiling water, second amounts of cooking oil and salt until tender but firm, about 11 to 13 minutes. Drain. Mix with meat. Turn into small roaster or extra large casserole.

Cover with cheese. Heat in 350°F (180°C) oven to melt cheese, about 10 to 15 minutes. Cover if heating longer. Serves 12.

Paré Pointer

She likes to make light of her age so she puts lots of candles on her birthday cake.

SAUCED MACARONI

Good mild flavor. Light color.

Olive oil (or cooking oil)	1 tbsp.	15 mL
Lean ground beef	1¼ lb.	625 g
Chopped onion	½ cup	125 mL
Condensed cream of mushroom soup	10 oz.	284 mL
Cottage cheese	1 cup	250 mL
Salt	1 tsp.	5 mL
Pepper	¼ tsp.	1 mL
Elbow macaroni	1 lb.	500 g
Boiling water	4 qts.	5 L
Cooking oil (optional)	1 tbsp.	15 mL
Salt	1 tbsp.	15 mL
Diced medium Cheddar cheese	¾ cup	175 mL

In olive oil, scramble-fry ground beef and onion until browned.

Add soup, cottage cheese, first amount of salt and pepper.

Cook macaroni in boiling water and second amount of salt until tender but firm, about 5 to 7 minutes. Drain. Add to meat mixture. Put into greased 3 quart (3.5 L) casserole.

Sprinkle with cheese. Cover. Bake in 350°F (180°C) oven for 20 minutes. Remove cover. Bake for about 10 minutes more. Serves 8.

SPAGHETTI AND SAUSAGE

You may prefer to double the meat in this rich looking casserole.

Sausage meat	½ lb.	225 g
Chopped onion	½ cup	125 mL
Tomato paste	5½ oz.	156 mL
Water	1½ cups	375 mL
Salt	½ tsp.	2 mL
Pepper	⅛ tsp.	0.5 mL
Garlic powder	¼ tsp.	1 mL
Spaghetti, broken in half	8 oz.	250 g
Boiling water	2½ qts.	3 L
Cooking oil (optional)	1 tbsp.	15 mL
Salt	2 tsp.	10 mL
Grated Swiss cheese or mozzarella	½ cup	125 mL

(continued on next page)

In saucepan scramble-fry sausage meat and onion to brown.

Add next 5 ingredients. Cover. Simmer for about 15 minutes.

In large uncovered saucepan cook spaghetti in boiling water, cooking oil and second amount of salt until tender but firm, about 11 to 13 minutes. Drain. Combine with sausage mixture. Put into greased 3 quart (3.5 L) casserole.

Cover with cheese. Heat in 350°F (180°C) oven to melt cheese, about 10 minutes. Use more cheese if you like. Serves 4.

MEXI NOODLES

A mild chili flavor accompanies this creamy good casserole with chicken or turkey.

Chopped onion	1 cup	250 mL
Butter or margarine	2 tbsp.	30 mL
Condensed cream of mushroom soup	10 oz.	284 mL
Condensed cream of chicken soup	10 oz.	284 mL
Water	1 cup	250 mL
Chopped green chilies	4 oz.	114 mL
Chicken bouillon powder	1 tbsp.	15 mL
Cooked chicken or turkey, cut up	2 cups	500 mL
Seasoned salt	½ tsp.	2 mL
Broad egg noodles	1 lb.	500 g
Boiling water	4 qts.	5 L
Cooking oil (optional)	1 tbsp.	15 mL
Salt	1 tbsp.	15 mL
Grated Monterey Jack cheese (or medium Cheddar cheese)	1 cup	250 mL

Sauté onion in butter in large saucepan or frying pan until soft and clear.

Add next 7 ingredients. Mix together. Heat through.

Cook noodles in boiling water, cooking oil and salt in uncovered Dutch oven until tender but firm, about 5 to 7 minutes. Drain. Combine with chicken mixture.

Stir in cheese to melt and serve. Makes 8½ cups (2 L).

Variation: Turn into greased 3 quart (3.5 L) casserole before adding cheese. Sprinkle cheese over top. Bake covered in 350°F (180°C) oven for about 30 minutes.

TRIPLE CHEESE TREAT

Rich and fabulous.

Lean ground beef	1½ lbs.	750 g
Chopped onion	½ cup	125 mL
Cooking oil	1 tbsp.	15 mL
Tomato paste	2 × 5½ oz.	2 × 156 mL
Water	1 cup	250 mL
Granulated sugar	2 tsp.	10 mL
Celery salt	½ tsp.	2 mL
Salt	1½ tsp.	7 mL
Pepper	¼ tsp.	1 mL
Garlic powder	¼ tsp.	1 mL
Cream cheese, softened	8 oz.	250 g
Sour cream	1 cup	250 mL
Cottage cheese	1 cup	250 mL
Grated green pepper	¼ cup	60 mL
Green onions, chopped	6	6
Medium egg noodles	8 oz.	250 g
Boiling water	2½ qts.	3 L
Cooking oil (optional)	1 tbsp.	15 mL
Salt	2 tsp.	10 mL
Grated Parmesan cheese	1 cup	250 mL
(or use twice as much grated medium Cheddar cheese)		

Scramble-fry ground beef and first amount of onion in first amount of cooking oil until browned.

Add next 7 ingredients. Stir. Bring to a boil. Set aside.

Beat cream cheese and sour cream together until smooth. Stir in cottage cheese, green pepper and green onions. Set aside.

In large uncovered saucepan cook noodles in boiling water, second amounts of cooking oil and salt until tender but firm, about 5 to 7 minutes. Drain.

Layer in greased 3 quart (3.5 L) casserole as follows:
1. One-half noodles
2. Cottage cheese mixture
3. One-half noodles
4. Meat mixture
5. Parmesan (or Cheddar) cheese

(continued on next page)

Bake covered in 350°F (180°C) oven for about 25 minutes. Uncover and continue to bake to brown cheese, about 15 minutes more. Serves 6 to 8.

Pictured on page 125.

JOHNNY MARZETTI

This is a variation of a recipe that was created by the owner of the Marzetti Restaurant. It was named after the owner's brother.

Butter or margarine	¼ cup	60 mL
Chopped onion	2 cups	500 mL
Sliced fresh mushrooms	1 cup	250 mL
Chopped celery	½ cup	125 mL
Small green pepper, chopped	1	1
Lean ground beef, broken up	1½ lb.	750 g
Condensed tomato soup	10 oz.	284 mL
Condensed cream of mushroom soup	10 oz.	284 mL
Tomato sauce	7½ oz.	213 mL
Salt	1 tsp.	5 mL
Pepper	¼ tsp.	1 mL
Large pasta shells (not jumbo)	8 oz.	250 g
Boiling water	2½ qts.	3 L
Cooking oil (optional)	1 tbsp.	15 mL
Salt	2 tsp.	10 mL
Grated medium Cheddar cheese	1½ cups	375 mL
Grated medium Cheddar cheese	1 cup	250 mL

Melt butter in large frying pan. Add next 5 ingredients. Fry and stir until vegetables are soft and no pink remains in meat.

Add tomato and mushroom soup. Stir in tomato sauce, first amount of salt and pepper. Turn into small roaster.

In large uncovered saucepan cook shells in water, cooking oil and second amount of salt until tender but firm, about 5 to 7 minutes. Drain. Add to roaster.

Add first amount of cheese. Stir to mix.

Sprinkle with remaining cheese. Bake covered in 350°F (180°C) oven for about 30 to 40 minutes until piping hot. Remove cover for a few minutes if cheese isn't melted. Serves 8 to 10.

SINGAPORE NOODLES

No need to go to Singapore for heat. Just make this. Serve accompanied with cold drinks. Actually this is not hot-hot. The second bite seems milder than the first. Good choice.

Cooking oil (part sesame gives good flavor)	¼ cup	60 mL
Garlic cloves, minced	4 - 6	4 - 6
Slivered ginger strips	2 tbsp.	30 mL
Water	2 qts.	2.5 L
Cooking oil	1 tbsp.	15 mL
Salt	2 tsp.	10 mL
Vermicelli nests	4 - 6	4 - 6
Cooked pork, chicken, shrimp or beef, cut up	2 cups	500 mL
Slivered green onions	⅓ cup	75 mL
Crushed red pepper (may be halved)	2 tsp.	10 mL
Oyster sauce	¼ cup	60 mL
Curry powder (may be halved)	3 tbsp.	50 mL
Soy sauce	2 tsp.	10 mL

Heat first amount of cooking oil in wok or frying pan. Add garlic and ginger. Cook until tender.

Heat water, second amount of cooking oil and salt in large uncovered saucepan until boiling. Add vermicelli. Make sure nests are covered with water. Turn off heat and let stand.

Add pork, green onion and red pepper to wok. Stir-fry until hot.

Add oyster sauce, curry powder and soy sauce. Stir and toss well to mix thoroughly. Drain noodles. Add and toss. May be served now or cover and place in 250°F (120°C) oven to hold until ready. Makes 2 good size plates if 4 nests are used, 3 plates if 6 are used.

Pictured on page 89.

Paré Pointer

The sandwich was actually invented when people discovered they could not live by bread alone.

Most attractive with two colors of cheese glistening on top. Rich creamy goodness.

MEAT MIXTURE

Lean ground beef	2 lbs.	1 kg
Chopped onion	¼ cup	60 mL
Cooking oil	1 tbsp.	15 mL
Seasoned salt	1½ tsp.	7 mL

TOMATO CHEESE MIXTURE

Condensed tomato soup	2 x 10 oz.	2 x 284 mL
Cream cheese, softened	8 oz.	250 g
Green onions, chopped	6	6
Sour cream	½ cup	125 mL
Broad egg noodles	12 oz.	375 g
Boiling water	3 qts.	4 L
Cooking oil (optional)	1 tbsp.	15 mL
Salt	2 tsp.	10 mL
Grated Cheddar cheese, medium or sharp	2 cups	500 mL

Mozzarella cheese, strips or grated

Meat Mixture: Scramble-fry ground beef and onion in cooking oil until browned. Sprinkle with seasoned salt. Stir well.

Tomato Cheese Mixture: In medium bowl mix soup, cream cheese, green onion and sour cream together well.

In uncovered Dutch oven cook noodles in boiling water, cooking oil and salt until tender but firm, about 5 to 7 minutes. Drain.

Assemble in greased 3 quart (3.5 L) casserole as follows:
1. One-half noodles
2. Meat mixture
3. One-half Cheddar cheese
4. Tomato cheese mixture
5. One-half noodles
6. One-half Cheddar cheese
7. Mozzarella cheese. Lay cheese in strips or sprinkle grated cheese mostly in center so some Cheddar cheese shows around the edge.

Cover. Bake in 350°F (180°C) oven for about 30 minutes until bubbling hot and cheese is melted. Serves 8.

Pictured on page 53.

PASTITSIO

This popular Greek dish has cinnamon and nutmeg in it. Very different and a treat to eat.

MEAT SAUCE

Lean ground beef	1½ lbs.	750 g
Chopped onion	1½ cups	375 mL
Margarine (butter browns too fast)	2 tbsp.	30 mL
Tomato sauce	7½ oz.	213 mL
Salt	1½ tsp.	7 mL
Pepper	¼ tsp.	1 mL
Red wine (or use alcohol-free red wine)	¼ cup	60 mL
Cinnamon	½ tsp.	2 mL
Nutmeg	½ tsp.	2 mL

WHITE SAUCE

Butter or margarine	½ cup	125 mL
All-purpose flour	½ cup	125 mL
Salt	1 tsp.	5 mL
Pepper	⅛ tsp.	0.5 mL
Milk	3 cups	750 mL
Grated Parmesan cheese	⅓ cup	75 mL
Prepared mustard	1 tsp.	5 mL
Chicken bouillon cube	1 × ⅕ oz.	1 × 6 g
Boiling water	1 cup	250 mL
Egg, lightly beaten	1	1

MACARONI

Elbow macaroni (about 4 cups, 900 mL)	1 lb.	500 g
Boiling water	4 qts.	5 L
Cooking oil (optional)	1 tbsp.	15 mL
Salt	1 tbsp.	15 mL
Eggs	3	3
Butter or margarine, softened	3 tbsp.	50 mL
Grated Parmesan cheese	½ cup	125 mL
Grated Parmesan cheese, for topping	½ cup	125 mL

Meat Sauce: Scramble-fry ground beef and onion in margarine in frying pan until browned. Drain off fat.

Add next 6 ingredients. Simmer uncovered for about 15 minutes. Set aside.

(continued on next page)

White Sauce: Melt butter in saucepan over medium heat. Mix in flour, salt and pepper. Stir in milk until it boils and thickens. Add cheese and mustard. Stir.

Dissolve bouillon cubes in boiling water. Add to sauce.

Stir some white sauce into egg then stir all of the egg into sauce. Remove from heat. Set aside.

Macaroni: In uncovered Dutch oven cook macaroni in boiling water, cooking oil and salt until tender but firm, about 5 to 7 minutes. Drain.

Beat eggs, butter and first amount of cheese with spoon in small bowl. Stir briskly into macaroni.

Assemble in layers in greased 9 × 13 inch (22 × 33 cm) pan as follows:
1. Two-thirds macaroni
2. Meat sauce
3. One-third macaroni
4. White sauce
5. Parmesan cheese for topping

Bake uncovered in 350°F (180°C) oven for 45 to 50 minutes until top is well browned. Cuts into 12 to 15 thick pieces.

Pictured on page 143.

REUBEN SPAGHETTI

Make this from leftover pasta or cook fresh pasta. Either way, this is a novel way to serve sauerkraut.

Cooked spaghetti	2½ cups	625 mL
Sauerkraut, drained	19 oz.	540 mL
Spaghetti Sauce, see page 78	1 cup	250 mL
Bacon slices	6	6

In greased 3 quart (3.5 L) casserole layer ½ spaghetti, ½ sauerkraut, ½ spaghetti and ½ sauerkraut.

Pour spaghetti sauce over all. Cut each bacon slice into 4 pieces. Lay bacon over top. Bake uncovered in 400°F (200°C) oven until heated through and bacon is crisp, about 25 minutes depending on thickness of bacon. Serves 4 to 6.

Note: Cook 8 oz. (250 g) spaghetti in boiling salted water until tender but firm to replace cooked spaghetti.

SHRIMP PASTA ROLL

A very different form of pasta. These rolls are very showy. Serve sliced with a sauce.

Butter or margarine	1 tbsp.	15 mL
Finely chopped celery	¼ cup	60 mL
Finely chopped onion	¼ cup	60 mL
Salt	¼ tsp.	1 mL
Cans of broken shrimp, drained and mashed	2 × 4 oz.	2 × 113 g
Chili sauce or seafood sauce	3 tbsp.	50 mL
Fine dry bread crumbs	4 tsp.	20 mL
Worcestershire sauce	½ tsp.	2 mL
Lemon juice	½ tsp.	2 mL
Dough from Fresh Egg Noodles, page 32		
Boiling water, to cover well		
Salt	2 tsp.	10 mL
CREAMY SAUCE		
Butter or margarine	¼ cup	60 mL
All-purpose flour	¼ cup	60 mL
Salt	¼ tsp.	1 mL
Pepper	⅛ tsp.	0.5 mL
Chicken bouillon powder	1 tsp.	5 mL
Milk	2 cups	500 mL

Melt butter in frying pan. Add celery, onion and first amount of salt. Sauté until soft. Remove from heat.

Add shrimp, chili sauce, bread crumbs, Worcestershire sauce and lemon juice. Stir.

Roll egg noodle dough quite thin into 2 rectangles, 9 × 12 inch (22 × 30 cm) each. Spread shrimp mixture over top to within 1 inch (2.5 cm) of the edges. Roll from short end like a jelly roll. Roll each roll up in a disposable dish cloth or cheesecloth. Tie ends.

Put into roaster or fish poacher containing boiling water and second amount of salt. Cook uncovered for about 30 minutes. Add more boiling water as needed to keep roll covered. Let stand 10 minutes or more before slicing and arranging in casserole.

Creamy Sauce: Melt butter in medium saucepan. Mix in flour, salt, pepper and bouillon powder. Stir in milk until it boils and thickens. Taste for salt and pepper, adding more if needed. Pour sauce over sliced pasta roll. Cover. Bake in 350°F (180°C) oven for about 30 minutes until hot. Serves 4 to 6.

(continued on next page)

CORNED BEEF PASTA ROLL: Mash 1 can, 12 oz. (341 mL), corned beef. Add 2 tsp. (10 mL) parsley flakes and 2 tbsp. (30 mL) milk or water. Spread over pasta instead of using shrimp mixture. Serve with Creamy Sauce.

Pictured without sauce on page 17.

BEEF NOODLE CASSEROLE

Get the feel and taste of eating lasagne in half the time. Yellow topped. Scrumptious.

Spaghetti	8 oz.	250 g
Boiling water	2½ qts.	3 L
Cooking oil (optional)	1 tbsp.	15 mL
Salt	2 tsp.	10 mL
Lean ground beef	½ lb.	250 g
Cooking oil	2 tsp.	10 mL
Spaghetti Sauce, see page 78	2½ cups	625 mL
Salt	½ tsp.	2 mL
Pepper	⅛ tsp.	0.5 mL
Butter or margarine	2 tbsp.	30 mL
All-purpose flour	2 tbsp.	30 mL
Milk	1 cup	250 mL
Velveeta cheese, diced (or use another mild soft process cheese)	1 cup	250 mL
Grated Parmesan cheese	3 tbsp.	50 mL

In large uncovered saucepan cook spaghetti in boiling water, first amounts of cooking oil and salt until tender but firm, about 11 to 13 minutes. Drain. Put into greased 9 × 9 inch (22 × 22 cm) pan.

Scramble-fry ground beef in second amount of cooking oil to brown. Drain.

Add spaghetti sauce, second amount of salt and pepper to meat. Simmer uncovered for 30 minutes. Pour over spaghetti.

Melt butter in saucepan. Mix in flour. Stir in milk until it boils and thickens.

Add both cheeses. Stir to melt. Pour over all. Bake uncovered in 350°F (180°C) oven for about 30 minutes until heated through and top is browning around edges. If it shows signs of browning too much before hot enough, cover. Cuts into 9 square pieces.

MUSHROOM LASAGNE

Although there is no meat in this, it has the familiar lasagne flavor. Mushrooms add their flavor as well. Excellent.

Lasagne noodles	10 - 12	10 - 12
Boiling water	4 qts.	5 L
Cooking oil (optional)	1 tbsp.	15 mL
Salt	1 tbsp.	15 mL
Butter or margarine	¼ cup	60 mL
Fresh mushrooms, sliced	1 lb.	454 g
Cream cheese, softened	8 oz.	250 g
Cottage cheese	2 cups	500 mL
Parsley flakes	1 tbsp.	15 mL
Salt	¾ tsp.	4 mL
Pepper	⅛ tsp.	0.5 mL
Garlic powder	⅛ tsp.	0.5 mL
Tomato sauce	2 x 7½ oz.	2 x 213 mL
Water	⅓ cup	75 mL
Basil	½ tsp.	2 mL
Oregano	¼ tsp.	1 mL
Grated Parmesan cheese	½ cup	125 mL
Grated mozzarella cheese	2 cups	500 mL

Cook noodles in next 3 ingredients in uncovered Dutch oven until tender but firm, about 14 to 16 minutes. Drain.

Melt butter in frying pan. Add mushrooms. Sauté until soft.

Mix cream cheese with cottage cheese, parsley, second amount of salt, pepper and garlic powder in bowl.

In separate bowl combine tomato sauce, water, basil and oregano. Mix well.

To assemble, layer as follows in greased 9 x 13 inch (22 x 33 cm) pan:
1. Layer of noodles
2. One-half mushrooms
3. One-half cream cheese mixture
4. One-half tomato sauce mixture
5. Layer of noodles
6. One-half mushrooms
7. One-half cream cheese mixture
8. One-half tomato sauce mixture
9. Parmesan cheese
10. Mozzarella cheese

(continued on next page)

Cover with greased foil so cheese won't stick to it. Bake in 350°F (180°C) oven for about 35 minutes. Remove foil and bake 10 to 15 minutes more. Let stand 10 minutes before cutting. Cuts into 12 pieces. Serves 8.

CHICKEN TETRAZZINI

Sherry gives this an elusive flavor. Delicious.

Butter or margarine	6 tbsp.	100 mL
Sliced fresh mushrooms	2 cups	500 mL
Chopped onion	1 cup	250 mL
Small green pepper, chopped	1	1
All-purpose flour	¼ cup	60 mL
Salt	1 tsp.	5 mL
Pepper	¼ tsp.	1 mL
Chicken bouillon powder	4 tsp.	20 mL
Water	2 cups	500 mL
Whipping cream	½ cup	125 mL
Sherry (or use alcohol-free sherry)	¼ cup	60 mL
Cooked chicken, cut in small bite size pieces	2 cups	500 mL
Medium egg noodles	8 oz.	250 g
Boiling water	2½ qts.	3 L
Cooking oil (optional)	1 tbsp.	15 mL
Salt	2 tsp.	10 mL
Grated Parmesan cheese, heavy sprinkle		

Melt butter in frying pan. Add mushrooms, onion and green pepper. Sauté until soft.

Sprinkle flour, first amount of salt, pepper and bouillon powder over top. Mix together. Stir in water until it boils and thickens. Add cream, sherry and chicken. Stir. Set aside.

In large uncovered saucepan cook noodles in boiling water, cooking oil and second amount of salt until tender but firm, about 5 to 7 minutes. Drain. Turn into greased 2 quart (2.5 L) casserole. Scoop chicken mixture over top.

Sprinkle with Parmesan cheese. Bake uncovered in 350°F (180°C) oven for 30 to 35 minutes until hot and lightly browned. Serves 6 to 8.

CREAMY TORTELLINI

Get the good meal without all the work to make the tortellini. Excellent.

Frozen tortellini	1 lb.	454 g
Boiling water	4 qts.	5 L
Light cream	2 cups	500 mL
Grated carrot	½ cup	125 mL
Dry onion flakes	2 tbsp.	30 mL
Dry celery leaves	1 tsp.	5 mL
Parsley flakes	1 tsp.	5 mL
Garlic powder	¼ tsp.	1 mL
Chicken bouillon powder	2 tsp.	10 mL
Salt	½ tsp.	2 mL
Pepper	⅛ tsp.	0.5 mL
Grated Parmesan cheese	¼ cup	60 mL

Cook tortellini in boiling water in uncovered Dutch oven for about 8 to 14 minutes until as tender as you prefer.

Measure next 9 ingredients into another saucepan. Bring to a boil over medium heat. Simmer slowly until carrot is cooked, about 5 minutes.

Combine tortellini with creamy mixture. Stir in Parmesan cheese. Additional Parmesan may be sprinkled over top. Serves 4.

1. Corned Pasta page 77
2. Trail Mix Salad page 23
3. Straw And Hay page 75
4. Wiener And Pasta Pot page 73

Begin with a white crust of spaghetti. Add a layer of cottage cheese. Cover with a reddish meat sauce and top with mozzarella cheese. Very attractive.

CRUST

Spaghetti	6 oz.	170 g
Boiling water	2½ qts.	3 L
Cooking oil (optional)	1 tbsp.	15 mL
Salt	2 tsp.	10 mL
Eggs	2	2
Grated Parmesan cheese	⅓ cup	75 mL
Butter or margarine, softened	2 tbsp.	30 mL

FILLING

Cottage cheese	1 cup	250 mL
Cooking oil	1 tbsp.	15 mL
Ground beef	1 lb.	500 g
Chopped onion	½ cup	125 mL
Chopped green pepper (optional)	¼ cup	60 mL
Canned tomatoes, cut up	1 cup	250 mL
Tomato paste	5½ oz.	156 mL
Granulated sugar	1 tsp.	5 mL
Oregano	1 tsp.	5 mL
Salt	½ tsp.	2 mL
Garlic powder	¼ tsp.	1 mL
Grated mozzarella cheese	1 cup	250 mL

Crust: Cook spaghetti in water, cooking oil and salt in uncovered Dutch oven until tender but firm, about 11 to 13 minutes. Drain.

Add eggs, cheese and butter. Mix together. Shape into crust in greased 10 inch (25 cm) pie plate.

Filling: Spread cottage cheese over bottom crust.

In cooking oil scramble-fry ground beef, onion and green pepper until no pink remains in meat and onion is soft.

Add tomatoes, tomato paste, sugar, oregano, salt and garlic powder. Mix together. Pour over cottage cheese. Bake uncovered in 350°F (180°C) oven for about 30 minutes.

Sprinkle with mozzarella cheese, using more if desired. Bake until cheese is melted, about 5 to 10 minutes more. Cuts into 6 wedges.

GNOCCHI

Tender little potato dumplings served with sauces below or Tomato Sauce, page 78. Make NYAK-kee soon.

Potatoes, unpeeled	2 lbs.	900 g
Boiling water		
Egg	1	1
Butter or margarine, softened	2 tsp.	10 mL
All-purpose flour	2¼ cups	500 mL
Salt	1 tsp.	5 mL
Boiling water	4 qts.	5 L
Salt	1 tbsp.	15 mL

Sauce of your choice

Cook potatoes in their skins in boiling water until tender. Drain. Peel. Mash until no lumps remain. Make a well in the center.

Put egg, butter, flour and first amount of salt into well of potato. Mix thoroughly to make a soft dough. Shape into long rolls as thick as a finger. Cut into 1 inch (2.5 cm) lengths.

Have a large pot of boiling water with second amount of salt ready. Add several gnocchi. When they rise to the top they should be cooked. Makes 10 to 11 dozen.

Serve with Super Sauce (page 39) or one of the following sauces.

Pictured on page 35.

CHEESE SAUCE WITH BACON

Butter or margarine	3 tbsp.	50 mL
All-purpose flour	3 tbsp.	50 mL
Salt	½ tsp.	2 mL
Pepper	⅛ tsp.	0.5 mL
Milk	2 cups	500 mL
Grated medium Cheddar cheese	1 cup	250 mL
Bacon slices, cooked and crumbled	4 - 6	4 - 6

Melt butter in saucepan over medium heat. Mix in flour, salt and pepper. Stir in milk and cheese until it boils and thickens. Pour over dumplings. Toss. Put into large shallow serving bowl.

Sprinkle with bacon. Serve.

QUICK BUTTER SAUCE: Pour about ¼ cup (60 mL) butter or margarine, melted, over dumplings. Toss gently. Put into bowl or platter. Sprinkle with grated Parmesan cheese.

Looks so special. This makes two rolls. May be halved easily. Slice and serve with a sauce.

Dough from Fresh Egg Noodles, see page 32		
Frozen chopped spinach, cooked and squeeze-drained	2 x 10 oz.	2 x 284 g
Ricotta cheese (or cottage cheese)	1 cup	250 mL
Grated Parmesan cheese	¼ cup	60 mL
Salt	1 tsp.	5 mL
Pepper	¼ tsp.	1 mL
Nutmeg	¼ tsp.	1 mL
Boiling water, to cover completely		
Salt	2 tsp.	10 mL
Super Sauce, page 39		
Grated Parmesan cheese		

Roll egg noodle dough quite thin into rectangle 9 × 12 inches (22 × 33 cm).

Mix next 6 ingredients together. Spread ½ over pasta up to 1 inch (2.5 cm) from edges. Roll up from short end like a jelly roll. Press ends and lengthwise edge to seal. Wrap in a piece of cheesecloth or disposable dish cloth. Tie ends with string. Repeat for second roll.

Boil in water and second amount of salt in uncovered fish poacher or roaster for about 30 minutes. Add more boiling water part way through cooking if needed to keep rolls covered. Drain. Let stand 10 minutes before slicing or chill it if you prefer. To serve, slice rolls. Arrange in greased casserole.

Pour Super Sauce (page 39) or Bolognese Sauce (page 34) over slices. Sprinkle with Parmesan cheese. Cover. Bake in 350°F (180°C) oven for about 30 minutes until hot. Serves 4 to 6.

Pictured without sauce on page 17.

ROLLED LASAGNE: Add ½ cup (125 mL) chopped cooked ham for color and flavor. Spread about 2 tbsp. (30 mL) filling over cooked lasagne strip that is cut in half crosswise. Roll. Repeat. Place seam sides down in some sauce with the rest of the sauce over top. Sprinkle with grated Parmesan cheese. Bake uncovered in 350°F (180°C) oven for about 15 minutes. Allow 2 rolls per person.

SPINACH STUFFED MANICOTTI

A cheezy filling topped with a zesty tomato sauce. Good.

Manicotti	20	20
Boiling water	4 qts.	5 L
Cooking oil (optional)	1 tbsp.	15 mL
Salt	1 tbsp.	15 mL
FILLING		
Italian sausage	1 lb.	454 g
Eggs	2	2
Grated mozzarella cheese	2 cups	500 mL
Cottage cheese	1 cup	250 mL
Grated Parmesan cheese	½ cup	125 mL
Dry bread crumbs	¼ cup	60 mL
Frozen chopped spinach, thawed	10 oz.	284 g
Salt, sprinkle		
Pepper, light sprinkle		
Nutmeg	⅛ tsp.	0.5 mL
Garlic powder	⅛ tsp.	0.5 mL
TOMATO SAUCE		
Stewed tomatoes	2 x 14 oz.	2 x 398 mL
Chopped onion	1 cup	250 mL
Bay leaf	1	1
Oregano	½ tsp.	2 mL
Basil	½ tsp.	2 mL
Tomato paste	5½ oz.	156 mL
Grated Parmesan cheese	¼ cup	60 mL

Cook manicotti in boiling water, cooking oil and salt in uncovered Dutch oven until barely tender, about 5 to 6 minutes. Rinse with cold water. Drain.

Filling: Remove casings from sausages. Scramble-fry meat. Drain and set aside.

Beat eggs lightly in bowl. Add next 9 ingredients. Add sausage meat. Mix together. Stuff manicotti. Set aside.

Tomato Sauce: Combine first 6 ingredients in saucepan. Bring to a boil. Simmer uncovered stirring often until sauce has boiled down and thickened, about 15 to 20 minutes. Discard bay leaf.

(continued on next page)

Spoon enough sauce into bottom of pan to cover. Use large enough pan to hold manicotti close together in single layer. Put manicotti in pan. Pour remaining sauce over manicotti. Bake covered in 350°F (180°C) oven for 20 minutes.

Sprinkle with Parmesan cheese. Bake 10 minutes more. Makes 20. Serve 2 or 3 per person.

Pictured on page 71.

QUICK CASSEROLE

Flavored with basil this is a large pasta casserole. Easy to make.

Lean ground beef	2 lbs.	1 kg
Medium onions, chopped	2	2
Cooking oil	1 tbsp.	15 mL
Spaghetti Sauce, see page 78	4 cups	1 L
Sliced mushrooms, drained	10 oz.	284 mL
Granulated sugar	1 tsp.	5 mL
Basil	1 tsp.	5 mL
Salt	2 tsp.	10 mL
Pepper	¼ tsp.	1 mL
Medium egg noodles	1 lb.	500 g
Boiling water	4 qts.	5 L
Cooking oil (optional)	1 tbsp.	15 mL
Salt	1 tbsp.	15 mL
Grated medium Cheddar cheese	2 cups	500 mL

Scramble-fry ground beef and onion in first amount of cooking oil until browned.

Add next 6 ingredients. Cover and simmer for about 15 minutes.

In uncovered Dutch oven cook noodles in boiling water, second amounts of cooking oil and salt until tender but firm, about 5 to 7 minutes. Drain. Combine with meat mixture. Turn into 3½ quart (4 L) greased casserole.

Sprinkle with cheese. Cover. Bake in 350°F (180°C) oven for 30 minutes. Remove cover. Bake about 15 minutes more. Serves 10 to 12.

EASY LASAGNE

Noodles are layered before cooking in this convenient dish. Delicious. A reprint from Company's Coming CASSEROLES which just has to be in Company's Coming PASTA.

MEAT SAUCE

Lean ground beef	1 lb.	500 g
Cooking oil	1 tbsp.	15 mL
Canned tomatoes, broken up	2 × 28 oz.	2 × 796 mL
Tomato sauce	7½ oz.	213 mL
Garlic salt	¼ tsp.	1 mL
Envelope spaghetti sauce mix	1	1

COTTAGE CHEESE MIXTURE

Cottage cheese	1 cup	250 mL
Egg	1	1
Grated Parmesan cheese	½ cup	125 mL
Grated mozzarella cheese	1½ cups	375 mL
Lasagne noodles, raw	12	12

Meat Sauce: Scramble-fry beef in cooking oil in large frying pan until brown.

Add tomatoes, tomato sauce, garlic salt and spaghetti sauce mix. Simmer slowly for 10 minutes. Stir occasionally.

Cottage Cheese Mixture: Mix cottage cheese, egg and Parmesan cheese together in small bowl.

To assemble, layer as follows in greased 9 × 13 inch (22 × 33 cm) pan:
1. Bit of meat sauce, enough to cover
2. Layer of raw noodles
3. One-half meat sauce
4. Cottage cheese mixture
5. Layer of raw noodles
6. One-half meat sauce
7. Mozzarella cheese

Cover tightly with greased foil. Bake in 350°F (180°C) oven for 1 hour or more, until noodles are tender. Let stand 10 minutes before serving. Cuts into 12 pieces.

Here's a chance to make your own when you have some time to devote to cooking.

DOUGH

Eggs	3	3
Olive oil (or cooking oil)	3 tbsp.	50 mL
All-purpose flour	3 cups	675 mL
Water	3-6 tbsp.	50-100 mL

FILLING

Lean ground beef	1 lb.	500 g
Finely chopped onion	⅓ cup	75 mL
Dry bread crumbs	⅓ cup	75 mL
Salt	1 tsp.	5 mL
Pepper	¼ tsp.	1 mL
Garlic powder	¼ tsp.	1 mL
Allspice	⅛ tsp.	0.5 mL
Frozen chopped spinach, cooked and squeezed to drain	10 oz.	284 g
Grated Parmesan cheese	½ cup	125 mL

Dough: Beat eggs until frothy. Add olive oil, flour and smallest amount of water. Mix well to form fairly firm ball. Add water as needed. If dough gets too wet, add more flour. It won't hurt the pasta. Knead on lightly floured surface until smooth. Cover.

Filling: Mix all ingredients together in bowl. If mixture seems too dry add 1 egg. Chill until needed.

Divide dough into 4 equal balls. Roll each ball into paper-thin sheet. On ½ of the sheet place 1 tsp. (5 mL) filling about 1 inch (2.5 cm) apart. Fold other half sheet over top. Press with fingers between each little mound to seal. Cut apart into 2 inch (5 cm) squares. Press each edge with fork to ensure they are sealed. Have a big pot of boiling water ready. Drop several into boiling water. Stir to make sure they aren't stuck to the bottom. When they float to the top they should be cooked, about 8 to 10 minutes. Drain. Serve Butter Sauce, Garlic Sauce or Meat Sauce (page 9) over ravioli. Makes about 4 dozen.

BUTTER SAUCE: Melt ¼ cup (60 mL) butter or margarine. Add to ravioli and toss. Sprinkle with grated Parmesan cheese.

GARLIC SAUCE: Melt ¼ cup (60 mL) butter or margarine. Mix ½ garlic clove, minced or ⅛ tsp. (0.5 mL) garlic salt or powder with melted butter before pouring over ravioli for an Italian touch. Make twice as much if you like lots of butter.

MEAT STUFFED MANICOTTI

These shells are stuffed with a zesty meat filling and covered with spaghetti sauce.

Manicotti	12	12
Boiling water	4 qts.	5 L
Cooking oil (optional)	1 tbsp.	15 mL
Salt	1 tbsp.	15 mL
Lean ground beef	2 lbs.	1 kg
Finely chopped onion	1 cup	250 mL
Finely chopped celery	1/3 cup	75 mL
Garlic clove, minced	1	1
Cooking oil	2 tbsp.	30 mL
Dry bread crumbs	1/2 cup	125 mL
Grated Parmesan cheese	1/4 cup	60 mL
Salt	2 tsp.	10 mL
Pepper	1/4 tsp.	1 mL
Eggs, fork beaten	2	2
Spaghetti Sauce, see page 78	4 cups	1 L
Butter or margarine	2 tbsp.	30 mL
Dry bread crumbs	1/2 cup	125 mL
Grated Parmesan cheese	1/4 cup	60 mL

In uncovered Dutch oven cook manicotti in boiling water, first amounts of cooking oil and salt until tender but firm, about 5 to 6 minutes. Drain. Rinse with cold water. Drain well.

Scramble-fry ground beef, onion, celery and garlic in remaining cooking oil in frying pan until browned. Remove from heat.

In small bowl combine next 5 ingredients. Mix well. Add to beef mixture. Stir together. Stuff manicotti.

Cover bottom of pan, large enough to hold manicotti in single layer, with a bit of spaghetti sauce. Arrange manicotti side by side in pan. Pour rest of sauce over top.

Melt butter in saucepan. Mix in remaining bread crumbs and cheese. Scatter over all. Bake covered in 400°F (200°C) oven for 30 to 40 minutes. Serves 6 people, 2 manicotti each.

These little gems are served in a creamy sauce. For a spicier dish, serve with a tomato sauce.

FILLING

Finely chopped cooked pork or chicken	1 cup	250 mL
Grated Parmesan cheese	3 tbsp.	50 mL
Egg	1	1
Salt	¼ tsp.	1 mL
Pepper, light sprinkle		

Mix all ingredients together well. Add a bit of water if needed to hold together.

TORTELLINI

All-purpose flour	2 cups	450 mL
Eggs	4	4
Salt	½ tsp.	2 mL
Boiling water	4 qts.	5 L

Mix together well to form a stiff dough. Divide into 4 balls. Roll on lightly floured surface. Cut into 2 inch (5 cm) circles. Place ¼ tsp. (1 mL) filling on each. Moisten edges with water, fold over, press to seal. Pull ends together away from curved sides. Use a touch of water to seal.

Cook uncovered in large pot of boiling water 8 to 10 minutes until tender. Makes about 4 dozen.

PARMESAN SAUCE

Whipping cream	1 cup	250 mL
Butter or margarine	1 tbsp.	15 mL
Grated Parmesan cheese	⅔ cup	150 mL
Chopped parsley	¼ cup	60 mL
Salt	⅛ tsp.	0.5 mL

Mix all ingredients together in saucepan. Bring to a slow simmer. Pour over tortellini. Serves 2.

Pictured on page 71.

Variation: Tortellini may be served with Marinara Sauce (page 37) and sprinkled with Parmesan cheese.

CAPPELLETI: These little hats use the same stuffing as ravioli or tortellini. Put filling in center of 2 inch (5 cm) squares. Fold over to form triangle. Bring 2 corners of long side up over your finger and pinch to seal. Boil like tortellini or ravioli.

POT STICKERS

These pork dumplings are cooked ahead of time. When ready to serve, brown one side only. Dip in your favorite sauce.

Ground pork	1 lb.	500 g
Dry bread crumbs	¼ cup	60 mL
Finely chopped green onion	⅓ cup	75 mL
Soy sauce	1 tbsp.	15 mL
Ginger	½ tsp.	2 mL
Garlic powder	¼ tsp.	1 mL
Salt	¾ tsp.	4 mL
Dough from Fresh Egg Noodles, see page 32		
Boiling water	4 qts.	5 L
Margarine or cooking oil	2 tbsp.	30 mL

Mix first 7 ingredients together in bowl.

Roll egg noodle dough quite thin. Cut into 3½ to 4 inch (8 to 10 cm) circles. Place 2 tsp. (10 mL) filling in center of wrapper. Dampen edges with water. Fold over. Press to seal.

In large uncovered pot of boiling water, drop in dumplings. Boil until they cook and rise, about 5 minutes. They will rise in about 1 minute but pork won't be cooked. Remove with slotted spoon to tray.

When ready to brown, heat margarine in frying pan. Fry dumplings until quite brown on 1 side only. Add margarine as needed. Do not turn. To serve, turn brown side up into bowl. Serve with Hotshot Sauce or your favorite sweet and sour sauce or soy sauce for dipping. Makes about 2 dozen.

HOTSHOT SAUCE

Tomato sauce	7½ oz.	213 mL
Dry onion flakes	1 tbsp.	15 mL
Cider vinegar	1 tbsp.	15 mL
Worcestershire sauce	½ tsp.	2 mL
Crushed red pepper	½ tsp.	2 mL
Ginger	¼ tsp.	1 mL
Salt	¼ tsp.	1 mL

Measure all ingredients into small saucepan. Heat slowly until it boils. Simmer for about ½ minute or so to blend flavors. Remove from heat. This will liven up any dish! Makes 1 cup (225 mL) hot spicy dip.

Pictured on page 89.

A kid's dish. A party dish.

Spaghetti (or use vermicelli or angel hair)	8 oz.	250 g
Boiling water	2½ qts.	3 L
Cooking oil (optional)	1 tbsp.	15 mL
Salt	2 tsp.	10 mL
Egg	1	1
Milk	½ cup	125 mL
Salt, sprinkle		
Pepper, sprinkle		
Tomato sauce	7¼ oz.	213 mL
Oregano	1 tsp.	5 mL
Basil	1 tsp.	5 mL
Grated mozzarella cheese	1 cup	250 mL
Margarine (butter browns too fast)	1 tbsp.	15 mL
Lean ground beef	½ lb.	250 g
Chopped onion	¼ cup	60 mL
Fresh mushrooms, sliced	6	6
Chopped green pepper	3 tbsp.	50 mL
Green and black olives, sliced	6	6
Grated Parmesan cheese, sprinkle		

Cook spaghetti in boiling water, cooking oil and first amount of salt in uncovered Dutch oven until tender but firm, about 11 to 13 minutes. Drain.

Add egg, milk, second amount of salt and pepper. Stir together. Pack into greased 12 inch (30 cm) pizza pan, raising edges slightly.

In small bowl mix tomato sauce, oregano and basil together. Spread over top.

Sprinkle with mozzarella cheese.

Melt margarine in frying pan. Add ground beef and onion. Scramble-fry until browned. Drain. Spoon over tomato sauce.

Sprinkle with sliced mushrooms, green pepper, olives and Parmesan cheese. Bake in 350°F (180°C) oven for about 30 minutes. Cover with foil for the first 20 minutes. Cuts into 4 to 6 wedges.

Note: If you prefer a more moist outer edge, fit strips of foil around the outside of pizza before cooking.

Pictured on page 53.

SPINACH LASAGNE

No meat in this. The green, red and white colors look so attractive. Good.

Lasagne noodles	10 - 12	10 - 12
Boiling water	4 qts.	5 L
Cooking oil (optional)	1 tbsp.	15 mL
Salt	1 tbsp.	15 mL
TOMATO MUSHROOM SAUCE		
Butter or margarine	2 tbsp.	30 mL
Chopped onion	1 cup	250 mL
Sliced fresh mushrooms	2 cups	500 mL
Tomato sauce	2 × 7½ oz.	2 × 213 mL
Tomato paste	5½ oz.	156 mL
Oregano	1 tsp.	5 mL
Salt	1 tsp.	5 mL
Granulated sugar	1 tsp.	5 mL
Basil	¼ tsp.	1 mL
SPINACH LAYER		
Cottage cheese	2 cups	500 mL
Egg	1	1
Frozen chopped spinach, thawed	10 oz.	284 mL
Salt, sprinkle		
Pepper, sprinkle		
Nutmeg, light sprinkle		
Grated Parmesan cheese	½ cup	125 mL
Grated mozzarella cheese	2 cups	500 mL

Cook noodles in boiling water, cooking oil and salt, uncovered, in large saucepan or Dutch oven until tender but firm, about 14 to 16 minutes. Drain.

Tomato Mushroom Sauce: Melt butter in large frying pan. Add onion. Sauté until soft and clear.

Add mushrooms. Sauté for 3 to 5 minutes until soft.

Add next 6 ingredients. Stir. Simmer slowly uncovered for 10 to 15 minutes.

Spinach Layer: Combine cottage cheese and egg in bowl. Add spinach with a sprinkle of salt, pepper and nutmeg.

(continued on next page)

To assemble, layer in greased 9 × 13 inch (22 × 33 cm) pan as follows:
1. Layer of noodles
2. One-half tomato mushroom sauce
3. Spinach
4. Layer of noodles
5. One-half tomato mushroom sauce
6. Parmesan cheese
7. Mozzarella cheese

Cover with greased foil. Bake in 350°F (180°C) oven for about 50 to 60 minutes. Let stand 10 minutes before cutting. Cuts into 12 pieces. Serves 8.

VEAL STUFFED TORTELLINI

Although this delectable dish serves only two, it can easily be increased.

Frozen veal stuffed tortellini	8 oz.	250 g
Boiling water	2½ qts.	3 L
Butter or margarine	¼ cup	60 mL
Chopped onion	½ cup	125 mL
Sliced fresh mushrooms	2 cups	500 mL
Whipping cream	1 cup	250 mL
Grated Parmesan cheese	¼ cup	60 mL
White wine (or alcohol-free wine)	1 tbsp.	15 mL
Dijon mustard	1 tsp.	5 mL
Salt	¼ tsp.	1 mL
Pepper	⅛ tsp.	0.5 mL

Cook tortellini in boiling water in uncovered Dutch oven for about 8 to 14 minutes until as tender as you prefer. Drain.

Heat butter in frying pan. Add onion and mushrooms. Sauté until soft. Add tortellini. Stir.

Add remaining ingredients. Bring to a boil, stirring. Add more wine if desired. Serves 2.

LASAGNE

An all time favorite. Handy to have this in the freezer.

Lasagne noodles	10 - 12	10 - 12
Boiling water	4 qts.	5 L
Cooking oil (optional)	1 tbsp.	15 mL
Salt	1 tbsp.	15 mL
MEAT SAUCE		
Lean ground beef	1 lb.	500 g
Cooking oil	2 tsp.	10 mL
Tomato sauce	3 x 7½ oz.	3 x 213 mL
Finely chopped green pepper	¼ cup	60 mL
Finely chopped onion	2 tbsp.	30 mL
Granulated sugar	1 tsp.	5 mL
Garlic salt	1 tsp.	5 mL
Oregano	½ tsp.	2 mL
Pepper	⅛ tsp.	0.5 mL
CHEESE MIXTURE		
Cottage cheese	2 cups	500 mL
Grated Parmesan cheese	½ cup	125 mL
Egg	1	1
Parsley flakes	1 tbsp.	15 mL
Salt	2 tsp.	10 mL
Pepper	⅛ tsp.	0.5 mL
Grated mozzarella cheese	2 cups	500 mL

In large uncovered saucepan or Dutch oven cook noodles in boiling water, cooking oil and salt until tender but firm, about 14 to 16 minutes. Drain.

Meat Sauce: Scramble-fry ground beef in cooking oil in large saucepan until browned.

Add next 7 ingredients to meat. Simmer slowly, uncovered, for 20 minutes.

Cheese Mixture: In small bowl combine cottage cheese, Parmesan cheese, egg, parsley flakes, salt and pepper. Mix well.

To assemble, layer in greased 9 x 13 inch (22 x 33 cm) pan as follows:
1. Layer of noodles
2. One-half meat sauce
3. Cheese mixture
4. Layer of noodles
5. One-half meat sauce
6. Mozzarella cheese

(continued on next page)

Bake uncovered in 350°F (180°C) oven about 45 to 55 minutes until nicely browned. Let stand 10 minutes before cutting. Cuts into 12 pieces. Serves 8.

PASTA PIZZA

Using packaged macaroni and cheese as a base, this makes a fun-for-all dish.

Packaged macaroni and cheese dinner	7¾ oz.	225 g
Eggs, lightly beaten	2	2
Spaghetti Sauce, see page 78	2 cups	500 mL
Chopped onion	1 cup	250 mL
Butter or margarine	2 tbsp	30 mL
Grated Cheddar cheese, medium or sharp	2 cups	500 mL
Sliced fresh mushrooms, to cover	8 - 12	8 - 12
Sliced processed meat such as summer sausage or pepperoni	10 oz.	275 g
Grated mozzarella cheese	2 cups	500 mL
Grated Parmesan cheese, sprinkle		
Pimiento-stuffed olives, sliced (optional)		

Prepare macaroni and cheese according to package directions. Add eggs and mix well. Press into greased 12 inch (30 cm) pizza pan. Bake in 350°F (180°C) oven for 10 minutes.

Spread spaghetti sauce over macaroni crust, keeping inside the edge about ½ inch (12 mm).

Sauté onion in butter until soft. Scatter over spaghetti sauce.

Layer remaining ingredients in order given. Bake 10 to 15 minutes more until hot and cheese is bubbly. Cut in wedges to serve 4 to 6.

Paré Pointer

He fed his horse dollar bills so it wouldn't buck.

NOODLE PANCAKES

Pasta patties that are quaint and flavorful. Delight the younger set.

Fine egg noodles	8 oz.	250 g
Boiling water	2½ qts.	3 L
Cooking oil (optional)	1 tbsp.	15 mL
Salt	2 tsp.	10 mL
Soy sauce	1 tbsp.	15 mL
Instant chicken bouillon powder	1 tbsp.	15 mL
Eggs, fork beaten	2	2
All-purpose flour	1 tbsp.	15 mL
Butter or margarine	1 tbsp.	15 mL

Cook noodles in boiling water, cooking oil and salt in uncovered Dutch oven until tender but firm, about 4 to 6 minutes. Drain. Return noodles to pot. Cool for 5 or 10 minutes.

Add soy sauce, bouillon powder, eggs and flour. Stir.

Heat butter in frying pan. Shape pasta into patties and brown both sides. Add more butter as needed. Serve warm as a hot pasta dish with main course. Makes 18 patties.

1. Chicken Noodle Soup page 19
2. Macaroni And Cheese Deluxe page 66
3. Herb Toast page 129
4. Triple Cheese Treat page 96

CHICKEN LASAGNE

Super good. You will love this even if you don't like lasagne. Excellent.

Lasagne noodles	10 - 12	10 - 12
Boiling water	4 qts.	5 L
Cooking oil (optional)	1 tbsp.	15 mL
Salt	1 tbsp.	15 mL
CHICKEN SAUCE		
Condensed cream of mushroom soup	10 oz.	284 mL
Condensed cream of chicken soup	10 oz.	284 mL
Finely chopped onion	1 cup	250 mL
Cottage cheese	1 cup	250 mL
Sour cream	½ cup	125 mL
Poultry seasoning	¼ tsp.	1 mL
Oregano	¼ tsp.	1 mL
Basil	¼ tsp.	1 mL
Sliced pimiento-stuffed or black olives (optional)	⅓ cup	75 mL
Grated Parmesan cheese	¾ cup	175 mL
Cooked chicken or turkey, cut up	4 cups	1 L
Shredded medium Cheddar cheese	2 cups	500 mL
Shredded mozzarella cheese	2½ cups	625 mL

Cook noodles in boiling water, cooking oil and salt in uncovered Dutch oven until tender but firm, about 14 to 16 minutes. Drain.

Chicken Sauce: Mix first 11 ingredients together in large bowl.

To assemble, layer in greased 9 x 13 inch (22 x 33 cm) pan as follows:
1. Layer of noodles
2. One-half chicken sauce
3. Cheddar cheese
4. Layer of noodles
5. One-half chicken sauce
6. Mozzarella cheese

Cover with greased foil. Bake in 350°F (180°C) oven for about 40 minutes. Remove foil. Bake approximately 10 minutes more to lightly brown cheese. Let stand 10 minutes before cutting. Cuts into 12 pieces. Serves 8.

MEXICAN LASAGNE

Try a different flavor. This has a good mild green chili taste. Good choice.

Lasagne noodles	10 - 12	10 - 12
Boiling water	4 qts.	5 L
Cooking oil (optional)	1 tbsp.	15 mL
Salt	1 tbsp.	15 mL

MEAT SAUCE

Lean ground beef	1½ lbs.	750 g
Cooking oil	1 tbsp.	15 mL
Canned tomatoes, mashed	14 oz.	398 mL
Tomato paste	5½ oz.	156 mL
Granulated sugar	2 - 3 tsp.	10 - 15 mL
Salt	1½ tsp.	7 mL
Pepper	¼ tsp.	1 mL
Garlic powder	¼ tsp.	1 mL

CHEESE SAUCE

Cream cheese, softened	4 oz.	125 g
Sour cream	½ cup	125 mL
Cottage cheese	1 cup	250 mL
Chopped green chilies	4 oz.	114 mL
Grated Parmesan cheese	⅓ cup	75 mL
Egg	1	1
Chopped green onions	2 tbsp.	30 mL
Grated Monterey Jack cheese	2 cups	500 mL

Cook noodles in boiling water, cooking oil and salt in uncovered Dutch oven until tender but firm, about 14 to 16 minutes. Drain.

Meat Sauce: Scramble-fry ground beef in cooking oil in large saucepan until browned.

Add tomatoes, tomato paste, sugar, salt, pepper and garlic powder. Stir. Bring to a boil. Simmer uncovered for 20 minutes, stirring occasionally.

Cheese Sauce: Beat cream cheese with sour cream in large bowl until smooth. Add cottage cheese, green chilies, Parmesan cheese, egg and onion. Stir.

(continued on next page)

128

To assemble, layer as follows in greased 9 × 13 inch (22 × 33 cm) pan:
1. Layer of noodles
2. One-half meat sauce
3. Cheese sauce
4. Layer of noodles
5. One-half meat sauce
6. Monterey Jack cheese

Cover with greased foil. Bake in 350°F (180°C) oven for 45 to 55 minutes. To brown cheese, remove foil halfway through. Let stand 10 minutes before cutting. Cuts into 12 pieces. Serves 8.

HERB TOAST

A good go-with for any pasta.

Butter or margarine, softened	½ cup	125 mL
Parsley flakes	1 tsp.	5 mL
Oregano	¼ tsp.	1 mL
Dill weed	¼ tsp.	1 mL
Garlic salt	¼ tsp.	1 mL
Grated Parmesan cheese	2 tbsp.	30 mL

French bread slices

Mix first 6 ingredients in small bowl until blended.

Spread mixture on both sides of each bread slice. Arrange on broiling pan. Broil both sides. Serve hot.

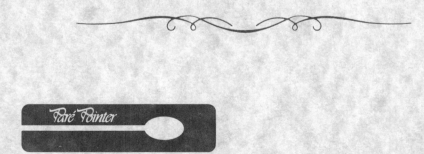

Pictured on page 125.

Paré Pointer

If you have a pig, a pool table and a tall tree, you have a pork-cue-pine.

SEAFOOD LASAGNE

A far cry from the usual lasagne. A bit expensive. Good flavor from the crab and shrimp.

Lasagne noodles	10 - 12	10 - 12
Boiling water	4 qts.	5 L
Cooking oil (optional)	1 tbsp.	15 mL
Salt	1 tbsp.	15 mL
CHEESE MIX		
Butter or margarine	2 tbsp.	30 mL
Chopped onion	1 cup	250 mL
Cream cheese, cut up	8 oz.	250 g
Cottage cheese	2 cups	500 mL
Egg	1	1
Salt	1 tsp.	5 mL
Pepper	¼ tsp.	1 mL
Basil	1 tsp.	5 mL
SEAFOOD MIX		
Condensed cream of mushroom soup	2 × 10 oz.	2 × 284 mL
Sherry (or alcohol-free sherry)	⅓ cup	75 mL
Cooked shrimp	¾ lb.	375 g
Crabmeat	½ lb.	250 g
Grated Parmesan cheese	⅓ cup	75 mL
Grated medium Cheddar cheese	1 cup	250 mL

Cook noodles in boiling water, cooking oil and salt in uncovered Dutch oven until tender but firm, about 14 to 16 minutes. Drain.

Cheese Mix: Melt butter in medium size saucepan. Add onion. Sauté until soft and clear.

Add cream cheese. Stir to melt. Remove from heat.

Add cottage cheese, egg, salt, pepper and basil. Stir together.

Seafood Mix: In medium size bowl combine soup, sherry, shrimp and crabmeat.

To assemble, layer as follows in greased 9 × 13 inch (22 × 33 cm) pan:
1. Layer of noodles
2. Cheese mix
3. Layer of noodles
4. Seafood mix
5. Parmesan cheese

(continued on next page)

Bake uncovered in 350ºF (180ºC) oven for about 45 minutes.

Sprinkle Cheddar cheese over top. Continue to bake until cheese melts and browns lightly, about 10 to 15 minutes. Let stand 10 minutes before cutting. Cuts into 12 pieces. Serves 8.

FETTUCCINE ALFREDO A LA MARINARA

Delicately flavored, delicate looking. A grand dish. Shrimp can be doubled if desired.

Fettuccine	**1 lb.**	**500 g**
Boiling water	**4 qts.**	**5 L**
Cooking oil (optional)	**1 tbsp.**	**15 mL**
Salt	**1 tbsp.**	**15 mL**
Butter or margarine	**½ cup**	**125 mL**
Whipping cream	**1 cup**	**250 mL**
Grated Parmesan cheese	**½ cup**	**125 mL**
Salt	**1 tsp.**	**5 mL**
Pepper	**¼ tsp.**	**1 mL**
Chopped parsley	**2 tbsp.**	**30 mL**
Canned small shrimp, drained, or other seafood	**4 oz.**	**113 g**

In uncovered Dutch oven cook fettuccine in water, cooking oil and first amount of salt until tender but firm, about 5 to 7 minutes. Drain. Return noodles to pot.

Combine butter and cream in saucepan over medium-low heat. Bring to a slow simmer.

Add cream mixture to noodles along with cheese, second amount of salt, pepper and parsley. Toss gently. Makes 9 cups (2.2 L).

Pictured on cover.

FETTUCCINE ALFREDO: Omit shrimp.

SHRIMP LINGUINI

This red creole style pasta is exceptional. Serve it soon.

Butter or margarine	¼ cup	60 mL
Green pepper, chopped	1	1
Chopped onion	½ cup	125 mL
Canned tomatoes, broken up	14 oz.	398 mL
Salt	1 tsp.	5 mL
Pepper	¼ tsp.	1 mL
Oregano	½ tsp.	2 mL
Basil	½ tsp.	2 mL
Garlic powder	1½ tsp.	7 mL
Cocktail size shrimp, fresh or frozen	½ lb.	250 g
Tomato sauce	7½ oz.	213 mL
Parsley flakes	2 tsp.	10 mL
Linguini	8 oz.	250 g
Boiling water	2½ qts.	3 L
Cooking oil (optional)	1 tbsp.	15 mL
Salt	2 tsp.	10 mL
Grated Parmesan cheese, heavy sprinkle		

Melt butter in saucepan. Add green pepper and onion. Sauté until soft.

Add next 6 ingredients. Simmer uncovered for about 20 to 30 minutes until juice is almost gone.

Add shrimp, tomato sauce and parsley. Simmer 15 minutes more.

Cook linguini in boiling water, cooking oil and second amount of salt in uncovered Dutch oven until tender but firm, about 5 to 7 minutes. Drain. Arrange linguini on warm platter or plates. Put shrimp mixture over top.

Sprinkle with Parmesan cheese. Serves 4.

Paré Pointer

You're only young once. Before long you'll need another excuse.

Great luncheon dish.

Butter or margarine	¼ cup	60 mL
Chopped green onion	½ cup	125 mL
Sliced fresh mushrooms	1 cup	250 mL
All-purpose flour	3 tbsp.	50 mL
Chicken bouillon powder	1 tbsp.	15 mL
Garlic powder	¼ tsp.	1 mL
Milk	1½ cups	375 mL
White wine (or alcohol-free wine)	¼ cup	60 mL
Medium egg noodles	8 oz.	250 g
Boiling water	2½ qts.	3 L
Cooking oil (optional)	1 tbsp.	15 mL
Salt	2 tsp.	10 mL
Cooked shrimp	2 cups	500 mL
Grated Swiss cheese	1 cup	250 mL
Grated Parmesan cheese	¼ cup	60 mL

Melt butter in frying pan or large saucepan. Add onion and mushrooms. Sauté until soft.

Mix in flour, bouillon powder and garlic powder. Add milk, stirring until it boils and thickens. Stir in wine. Remove from heat.

Cook noodles in boiling water, cooking oil and salt in uncovered Dutch oven until tender but firm, about 5 to 7 minutes. Drain. Combine with sauce.

Add shrimp. Toss together. Turn into greased 2 quart (2.5 L) casserole.

Sprinkle Swiss cheese over top, then Parmesan. Bake uncovered in 350°F (180°C) oven for 25 to 30 minutes until hot and golden. Serves 4.

Paré Pointer

At last — a good use for hippies. They keep your stockings up.

TUNA NOODLES PARMESAN

An easy casserole with gourmet overtones. Contains yogurt. Serve with a salad, rolls and perhaps a vegetable. Cheezy orange color topping.

Medium egg noodles	8 oz.	250 g
Boiling water	2½ qts.	3 L
Cooking oil (optional)	1 tbsp.	15 mL
Salt	2 tsp.	10 mL
Condensed cream of mushroom soup	10 oz.	284 mL
Yogurt	1 cup	250 mL
Chopped green onion	¼ cup	60 mL
Flaked tuna, drained	7 oz.	198 g
Grated Parmesan cheese	½ cup	125 mL
Sliced mushrooms with juice	10 oz.	284 mL
Sliced green pimiento-stuffed olives	⅓ cup	75 mL
Salt	½ tsp.	2 mL
Grated medium Cheddar cheese	¾ cup	175 mL
Paprika, sprinkle		

Cook noodles in boiling water, cooking oil and first amount of salt in uncovered Dutch oven until tender but firm, about 5 to 7 minutes. Stir occasionally.

Meanwhile, combine next 8 ingredients together in large bowl. Drain noodles and add them to mixture. Mix. Turn into 2½ to 3 quart (3 to 3.5 L) greased casserole.

Spread cheese over top. Sprinkle with paprika. Bake covered in 350°F (180°C) oven for about 30 minutes. Remove cover and bake 10 minutes more to brown. Serves 6.

BUSY DAY PASTA

A snap to make. A snap to eat.

Packaged macaroni and cheese dinner	7¾ oz.	225 g
Flaked tuna, drained	7 oz.	198 g

Prepare macaroni and cheese according to package directions.

Add tuna. Mix well. Heat through and serve. Makes 3 cups (700 mL).

LINGUINI WITH CLAM SAUCE

A familiar pasta to most, this is very light on the garlic. Add freely if you choose.

Linguini	1 lb.	500 g
Boiling water	4 qts.	5 L
Cooking oil (optional)	1 tbsp.	15 mL
Salt	1 tbsp.	15 mL
Butter or margarine	2 tbsp.	30 mL
Olive oil (or cooking oil)	2 tbsp.	30 mL
Chopped onion	½ cup	125 mL
Garlic clove, minced (or ¼ tsp., 1 mL, garlic powder)	1	1
Juice, drained from clams		
Salt	¼ tsp.	1 mL
Pepper, light sprinkle		
Chopped parsley (or 1 tsp., 5 mL, flakes)	2 tbsp.	30 mL
Baby clams, drained	2 x 5 oz.	2 x 142 g
White wine (or alcohol-free wine)	1 tbsp.	15 mL
Grated Parmesan cheese, sprinkle		

In uncovered Dutch oven cook linguini in boiling water, cooking oil and first amount of salt until tender but firm, about 11 to 13 minutes. Drain.

Toss linguini with butter.

Meanwhile, in olive oil, sauté onion and garlic until soft.

Add clam juice, second amount of salt, pepper and parsley. Simmer until volume of juice is reduced to ½ quantity.

Add clams and wine, adding more wine to taste. Heat through. Place linguini on warm platter. Pour clam sauce over top.

Sprinkle with Parmesan cheese. Serves 8.

Paré Pointer

Too many people pray for rain then complain about the mud.

SHRIMP SPAGHETTI

Creamy shrimp with spaghetti — looks appetizing!

Spaghetti	8 oz.	250 g
Boiling water	2½ qts.	3 L
Cooking oil (optional)	1 tbsp.	15 mL
Salt	2 tsp.	10 mL
Butter or margarine	¼ cup	60 mL
Fresh sliced mushrooms	1 cup	250 mL
Chopped green onion	¼ cup	60 mL
Frozen shrimp, thawed	½ lb.	250 g
All-purpose flour	¼ cup	60 mL
Salt	1 tsp.	5 mL
Pepper (white is best)	¼ tsp.	1 mL
Paprika	¼ tsp.	1 mL
Milk	2 cups	500 mL
Grated medium Cheddar cheese	1 cup	250 mL
White wine (or alcohol-free wine)	2 tbsp.	30 mL
Grated Parmesan cheese	3 tbsp.	50 mL

Cook spaghetti in boiling water, cooking oil and first amount of salt in uncovered Dutch oven until tender but firm, about 11 to 13 minutes. Drain.

Meanwhile, melt butter in frying pan or large saucepan. Add mushrooms and onion. Sauté until soft.

Add shrimp. Sauté until a pinkish color, about 5 minutes.

Sprinkle flour, second amount of salt, pepper and paprika over top. Mix in. Add milk. Stir until it boils and thickens.

Add Cheddar cheese and wine. Add drained pasta. Stir to mix. Turn out onto warm platter.

Sprinkle with Parmesan cheese. Serve. Makes 5 cups (1.2 L).

Paré Pointer

Don't worry about dying. That's the last thing you'll do.

LINGUINI WITH RED CLAM SAUCE

Lots of tomato sauce with this instead of the more common light colored sauce.

Olive oil (or cooking oil)	3 tbsp.	50 mL
Chopped onion	1 cup	250 mL
Garlic cloves, minced	2	2
Canned tomatoes, broken up	28 oz.	796 mL
Granulated sugar	1 tsp.	5 mL
Salt	1 tsp.	5 mL
Pepper	¼ tsp.	1 mL
Oregano	½ tsp.	2 mL
Basil	1 tsp.	5 mL
Tomato paste	5½ oz.	156 mL
Red wine (or alcohol-free wine)	½ cup	250 mL
Juice, drained from clams		
Chopped parsley	1 tbsp.	15 mL
Baby clams, drained	2 x 5 oz.	2 x 142 g
Linguini	1 lb.	500 g
Boiling water	4 qts.	5 L
Cooking oil (optional)	1 tbsp.	15 mL
Salt	1 tbsp.	15 mL
Butter or margarine, melted	¼ cup	60 mL
Grated Parmesan cheese, for topping		

Heat olive oil in large saucepan. Add onion and garlic. Sauté until soft.

Add next 10 ingredients. Stir together. Simmer uncovered for 10 minutes.

Add clams. Heat through.

In uncovered Dutch oven, cook linguini in boiling water, cooking oil and second amount of salt until tender but firm, about 11 to 13 minutes. Drain.

Add melted butter and toss. Arrange linguini on 4 warmed plates.

Divide clam sauce over top of each serving. Sprinkle with cheese.

Paré Pointer

In a run down neighborhood you can find poor quarters for good dollars.

SEAFOOD PASTA

A festive dish containing shrimp and scallops.

Fettuccine, white or green	1 lb.	500 g
Boiling water	4 qts.	5 L
Cooking oil (optional)	1 tbsp.	15 mL
Salt	1 tbsp.	15 mL
Butter or margarine	¼ cup	60 mL
Frozen shrimp, thawed	1 lb.	500 g
Frozen scallops, thawed, halved if large	1 lb.	500 g
Chopped green onion	¼ cup	60 mL
Seasoned salt	1 tsp.	5 mL
Sour cream	2 cups	500 mL
Pepper, light sprinkle		
Parmesan cheese		

Cook fettuccine in boiling water, cooking oil and salt in uncovered Dutch oven until tender but firm, about 5 to 7 minutes. Drain.

Meanwhile, melt butter in large frying pan. Add shrimp, scallops, onion and seasoned salt. Sauté until scallops turn white and shrimp turn pinkish, about 5 minutes.

Stir sour cream into noodles. Sprinkle with pepper. Add seafood mixture. Toss. Pass grated Parmesan cheese on the side. Serves 6 to 8.

CRAB NOODLES

A delicately flavored pasta. Serve this with ease.

Fettuccine	8 oz.	250 g
Boiling water	2½ qts.	3 L
Cooking oil (optional)	1 tbsp.	15 mL
Salt	2 tsp.	10 mL
Butter or margarine	¼ cup	60 mL
Crab, cartilage removed	5 oz.	142 g
Garlic powder	¼ tsp.	1 mL
Whipping cream	½ cup	125 mL
Grated Parmesan cheese	½ cup	125 mL
Salt	½ tsp.	2 mL
Pepper	¼ tsp.	1 mL
Chopped parsley, for garnish		

(continued on next page)

Cook fettuccine in boiling water, cooking oil and first amount of salt in uncovered Dutch oven until tender but firm, about 5 to 7 minutes. Drain. Return to pot.

In small saucepan heat butter, crab and garlic powder. Add cream, cheese, second amount of salt and pepper. Heat. Pour over drained noodles. Toss. Turn into serving bowl.

Garnish with parsley. Makes 5 cups (1.2 L).

NOODLES WITH SHRIMP

Light color. Flavorful creamy sauce. A good way to serve shrimp.

Medium egg noodles	8 oz.	250 g
Boiling water	2½ qts.	3 L
Cooking oil (optional)	1 tbsp.	15 mL
Salt	2 tsp.	10 mL
Olive oil (or cooking oil)	¼ cup	60 mL
Green onions, sliced	6	6
Sliced fresh mushrooms	2 cups	500 mL
Red pepper, chopped	1	1
Garlic clove, minced (optional)	1	1
Salt	½ tsp.	2 mL
Dill weed	½ tsp.	2 mL
Frozen shrimp, thawed	1 lb.	500 g
Whipping cream	1 cup	250 mL
Grated Parmesan cheese	1 cup	250 mL

Cook noodles in boiling water, cooking oil and first amount of salt in uncovered Dutch oven until tender but firm, about 5 to 7 minutes.

While noodles are cooking, heat olive oil in frying pan. Add onion, mushrooms, red pepper, garlic, second amount of salt and dill weed. Sauté until onion is soft.

Add shrimp. Sauté until they turn pink, about 5 minutes.

Drain noodles. Add cream and cheese. Heat through. Add shrimp mixture. Toss together. Serves 2 to 4.

TUNA AND PASTA

Creamy and saucy with tomato added. Good.

Rotini or other pasta	8 oz.	250 g
Boiling water	2½ qts.	3 L
Cooking oil (optional)	1 tbsp.	15 mL
Salt	2 tsp.	10 mL
Butter or margarine	2 tbsp.	30 mL
All-purpose flour	2 tbsp.	30 mL
Milk	1 cup	250 mL
Canned tomatoes, broken up	1 cup	250 mL
Salt	½ tsp.	2 mL
Flaked tuna, drained	7 oz.	198 g
Grated medium Cheddar cheese	1 cup	250 mL

Cook rotini in boiling water, cooking oil and first amount of salt in uncovered Dutch oven until tender but firm, about 10 to 13 minutes. Drain.

Melt butter in large saucepan. Mix in flour. Add milk. Stir until it boils and thickens.

Add remaining ingredients along with pasta. Mix and heat through. Makes a generous 4 cups (1 L).

NOODLES WITH SALMON

Make this from supplies on the shelf. Creamy good.

Medium egg noodles	8 oz.	250 g
Boiling water	2½ qts.	3 L
Cooking oil (optional)	1 tbsp.	15 mL
Salt	2 tsp.	10 mL
Salmon, drained, skin and round bones removed	7¾ oz.	220 g
Salt, sprinkle		
Pepper, sprinkle		
Condensed cream of mushroom soup	10 oz.	284 mL
Water	1¼ cups	300 mL
Dry bread crumbs	½ cup	125 mL
Butter or margarine	2 tbsp.	30 mL

(continued on next page)

Cook noodles in boiling water, cooking oil and first amount of salt in uncovered Dutch oven until tender but firm, about 5 to 7 minutes. Stir occasionally. Drain. Put ½ noodles into greased 2 quart (2.5 L) casserole.

Layer salmon over top. Sprinkle with salt and pepper. Add remaining noodles over top of salmon.

Mix soup with water. Pour over top of noodles.

Mix bread crumbs with butter in small saucepan over low heat. Sprinkle over all. Bake uncovered in 350°F (180°C) oven until hot and bubbly, about 25 minutes. Serves 4.

DATE WON TONS

Little sweet bundles wrapped like candy kisses.

Pitted dates, chopped	8 oz.	250 g
Finely chopped walnuts	½ cup	125 mL
Brown sugar, packed	½ cup	125 mL
Water	½ cup	125 mL
Lemon juice	1 tsp.	5 mL
Vanilla	½ tsp.	2 mL
Won ton wrappers	1 lb.	454 g
Fat for deep-frying		
Icing (confectioner's) sugar		

Combine first 6 ingredients in saucepan. Bring to a boil. Simmer slowly, stirring often until thick. Mixture should stay in a small heap when spooned onto won ton wrappers.

Place ½ tsp. (2 mL) of date filling in center of outside edge, nearest to you, of won ton wrapper. Dampen other 3 edges with water. Roll up like a jelly roll. Press to twist open ends to seal. Deep-fry in 375°F (190°C) hot fat until golden brown. Drain on paper towels. Cool.

To serve, sift icing sugar over top. Makes about 5 dozen won tons.

Pictured on page 143.

NOODLE COOKIES

Leftover noodles will save one step in making these. A bit time consuming but it is a novelty to make your own from scratch.

Fine egg noodles	4 oz.	125 g
Boiling water	1½ qts.	2 L
Cooking oil (optional)	2 tsp.	10 mL
Salt	1½ tsp.	7 mL
Fat for deep-frying		
Butter or margarine	2 tbsp.	30 mL
Semisweet chocolate chips	1 cup	250 mL
Chopped walnuts	½ cup	125 mL

Cook noodles in boiling water, cooking oil and salt in uncovered saucepan until tender but firm, about 5 to 7 minutes. Drain. Rinse with cold water. Drain well.

Be sure to drain noodles well as the wetter they are the more the fat will boil up and splatter. Deep-fry noodles in 375°F (190°C) hot fat until golden. Drain on paper towels.

Combine butter, chocolate chips and walnuts in large saucepan over low heat. Melt, stirring often. Add crisp deep-fried noodles. Stir to coat. Drop in little piles on trays or plates covered with waxed paper. Chill. Makes about 20 cookies.

APRICOT NOODLE PUDDING

About the best pasta dessert you can eat.

Medium egg noodles	8 oz.	250 g
Boiling water	2½ qts.	3 L
Cooking oil (optional)	1 tbsp.	15 mL
Salt	2 tsp.	10 mL
Cream cheese, softened	8 oz.	250 g
Butter or margarine	¼ cup	60 mL
Granulated sugar	½ cup	125 mL
All-purpose flour	1 tbsp.	15 mL
Eggs	3	3
Milk	1 cup	250 mL
Strained apricots (baby food)	2 x 7½ oz.	2 x 213 mL

TOPPING

Butter or margarine	¼ cup	60 mL
Graham cracker crumbs	1 cup	250 mL
Brown sugar, packed	¼ cup	60 mL

Cook noodles in boiling water, cooking oil and salt in uncovered Dutch oven until tender but firm, about 5 to 7 minutes. Drain. Rinse with cold water. Drain well.

Beat cream cheese, butter, sugar and flour together in bowl until smooth. Beat in eggs 1 at a time. Add milk, apricots and noodles. Stir. Turn into 3 quart (3.5 L) casserole.

Topping: Melt butter in small saucepan. Mix in crumbs and sugar. Scatter over top. Bake uncovered in 350°F (180°C) oven to brown topping, about 15 minutes. Serves 8 to 10.

Pictured on page 71.

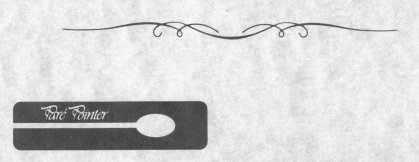

Paré Pointer

She is such a pessimist. All she would look for on a silver platter is tarnish.

PASTA TIDBITS

Filled with a chocolate-cheese mixture. This also lends itself to any other fruit filling of your choice. Try the apricot filling as well.

PASTA DOUGH

All-purpose flour	1 cup	250 mL
Granulated sugar	2 tbsp.	30 mL
Salt	$\frac{1}{16}$ tsp.	0.5 mL
Egg yolk	1	1
Butter or margarine, melted	6 tbsp.	100 mL
Lemon juice	1 tsp.	5 mL

Measure flour, sugar and salt into bowl. Mix together. Make a well in center.

Put egg yolk, butter and lemon juice into well. Mix until all dry ingredients are absorbed. Add more melted butter if needed to moisten. Dough should be soft. Chill for 2½ to 3 hours.

FILLING

Cream cheese, softened	4 oz.	125 g
Granulated sugar	$\frac{1}{3}$ cup	75 mL
Semisweet chocolate chips	$\frac{1}{3}$ cup	75 mL

Fat for deep-frying
Icing (confectioner's) sugar

Beat cream cheese and sugar in small bowl until smooth.

Melt chocolate chips in saucepan over low heat. Combine with cheese-sugar mixture. Chill about 1 hour.

Roll dough paper thin on lightly floured surface. Cut into 2½ inch (6.5 cm) circles. Place a teaspoonful of filling in center of each circle. Dampen edges with water. Fold over. Press to seal.

Drop into hot fat 375°F (190°C). Deep-fry until golden. Drain on paper towels. Sift icing sugar over top before serving. Makes about 3½ dozen.

APRICOT FILLING

Dried apricots, chopped	½ cup	125 mL
Dates, chopped	¼ cup	60 mL
Coconut	¼ cup	60 mL
Graham cracker crumbs	¼ cup	60 mL
Granulated sugar	3 tbsp.	50 mL
Orange or apple juice	1½ tbsp.	25 mL
Lemon juice	1 tsp.	5 mL

(continued on next page)

Put apricots and dates through grinder. Combine with remaining ingredients. Mix together well. Add a bit more juice if too dry. Use to fill Pasta Tidbits.

Pictured on page 143.

APPLE NOODLE DESSERT

Good apple and cinnamon flavor.

Broad egg noodles, broken up	8 oz.	250 g
Boiling water	2½ qts.	3 L
Cooking oil (optional)	1 tbsp.	15 mL
Salt	2 tsp.	10 mL
Peeled and sliced cooking apples	2 cups	500 mL
Butter or margarine	3 tbsp.	50 mL
Brown sugar	3 tbsp.	50 mL
Cottage cheese	1 cup	250 mL
Eggs	4	4
Granulated sugar	½ cup	125 mL
Milk	1½ cups	375 mL
Sour cream	½ cup	125 mL
Vanilla	1 tsp.	5 mL
Cinnamon	1 tsp.	5 mL
Raisins or currants	½ cup	125 mL

Cook noodles in boiling water, cooking oil and salt in uncovered Dutch oven until tender but firm, about 5 to 7 minutes. Drain. Rinse with cold water. Drain well.

Sauté apples in butter and brown sugar in frying pan until soft.

Beat cottage cheese in mixing bowl. Add eggs 1 at a time beating after each addition. Mix in remaining ingredients. Add noodles and apple mixture. Toss together carefully. Put into greased 3 quart (3.5 L) casserole. Bake uncovered in 350°F (180°C) oven for 40 to 50 minutes. Makes 8 good size servings.

MOCK BREAD PUDDING

A very great similarity to the real thing.

Broad egg noodles, broken up	8 oz.	250 g
Boiling water	2½ qts.	3 L
Cooking oil (optional)	1 tbsp.	15 mL
Salt	2 tsp.	10 mL
Eggs	2	2
Milk	2 cups	500 mL
Butter or margarine, melted	¼ cup	60 mL
Brown sugar, packed	½ cup	125 mL
Raisins or currants	1 cup	250 mL
Vanilla	1 tsp.	5 mL
Salt	¾ tsp.	4 mL
Cinnamon	½ tsp.	2 mL

Cook noodles in boiling water, cooking oil and first amount of salt in uncovered Dutch oven until tender but firm, about 5 to 7 minutes. Drain. Rinse with cold water. Drain well.

Beat eggs until frothy in bowl. Add remaining ingredients. Mix together. Add noodles. Stir. Turn into greased 2 quart (2 L) casserole. Bake uncovered in 350°F (180°C) oven for 30 to 40 minutes until set. Let stand for 20 to 30 minutes before serving. The noodles will absorb the liquid. Serves 6 to 8.

MOCK RICE PUDDING

No pre-cooking of pasta. Just place in the oven and bake.

Alphabets or tiny pasta	1 cup	250 mL
Milk	2 cups	500 mL
Granulated sugar	¼ cup	60 mL
Raisins	2 tbsp.	30 mL
Vanilla	½ tsp.	2 mL

In medium size bowl mix all ingredients together. Put into 2 quart (2.5 L) casserole. Bake uncovered in 350°F (180°C) oven for about 45 minutes. Stir well after 20 minutes of baking. Let stand 10 minutes before serving in fruit nappies. Pass cream or milk to pour over top. Serves 6.

This is a creamy pudding with a cinnamon flavored topping. Contains pineapple and raisins.

Broad egg noodles, broken up	8 oz.	250 g
Boiling water	2½ qts.	3 L
Cooking oil (optional)	1 tbsp.	15 mL
Salt	2 tsp.	10 mL
Eggs	4	4
Granulated sugar	½ cup	125 mL
Butter or margarine, melted	½ cup	125 mL
Sour cream	1 cup	250 mL
Cottage cheese	1 cup	250 mL
Milk	1 cup	250 mL
Vanilla	2 tsp.	10 mL
Salt	¾ tsp.	4 mL
Raisins or currants	½ cup	125 mL
Crushed pineapple, drained	14 oz.	398 mL
TOPPING		
Corn flake crumbs	1 cup	250 mL
Granulated sugar	½ cup	125 mL
Cinnamon	1 tsp.	5 mL

Cook noodles in boiling water, cooking oil and first amount of salt in uncovered Dutch oven until tender but firm, about 5 to 7 minutes. Drain. Rinse with cold water. Drain well.

Beat eggs until frothy in large mixing bowl. Add sugar, butter, sour cream, cottage cheese, milk, vanilla and second amount of salt. Mix.

Add raisins and pineapple. Add noodles. Mix together. Put into greased 3 quart (3.5 L) casserole.

Topping: Mix all 3 ingredients together well. Sprinkle over top. Bake uncovered in 350°F (180°C) oven for 30 to 40 minutes. Serves 8 generously.

Approximate measures of 8 oz. (250 g) popular pasta.

Spaghetti
— 1½ inch (4 cm) in diameter (a tightly held fist full)

Fine egg noodles
— 4 cups (1 L)

Medium egg noodles
— 3⅓ cups (825 mL)

Broad egg noodles
— 3 cups (750 mL)

Macaroni
— 2 cups (500 mL)

Ditali
— 2⅓ cups (575 mL)

Tubettini
— 1⅓ cups (325 mL)

Stars
— 1⅓ cups (325 mL)

Alphabets
— 1¼ cups (300 mL)

Wagon Wheels
— 2⅔ cups (650 mL)

Bows
— 4 cups (1 L)

Cappelletti
— 2⅔ cups (650 mL)

Fusili
— 2⅔ cups (650 mL)

Rotini
— 3½ cups (800 mL)

Spaccatella
— 3½ cups (850 mL)

Tiny Shells
— 2 cups, scant (500 mL)

Large Shells
— 4 cups, scant (500 mL)

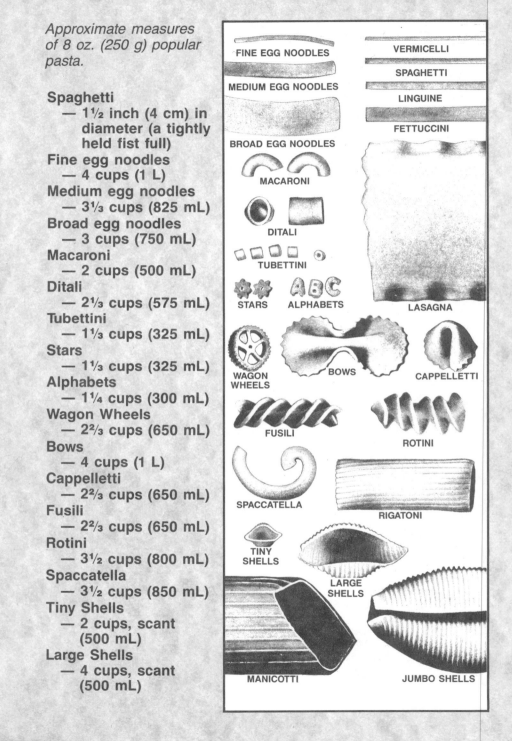

FINE EGG NOODLES

MEDIUM EGG NOODLES

BROAD EGG NOODLES

MACARONI

DITALI

TUBETTINI

STARS ALPHABETS

VERMICELLI

SPAGHETTI

LINGUINE

FETTUCCINI

LASAGNA

WAGON WHEELS BOWS CAPPELLETTI

FUSILI ROTINI

SPACCATELLA RIGATONI

TINY SHELLS LARGE SHELLS

MANICOTTI JUMBO SHELLS

Throughout this book measurements are given in conventional and metric measure. To compensate for differences between the two measurements due to rounding, a full metric measure is not always used.

The cup used is the standard 8 fluid ounce.

Temperature is given in degrees Fahrenheit and Celsius.

Baking pan measurements are in inches and centimetres, as well as quarts and litres. An exact conversion is given below as well as the working equivalent.

Spoons	Exact Conversion	Standard Metric Measure
¼ teaspoon	1.2 millilitres	1 millilitre
½ teaspoon	2.4 millilitres	2 millilitres
1 teaspoon	4.7 millilitres	5 millilitres
2 teaspoons	9.4 millilitres	10 millilitres
1 tablespoon	14.2 millilitres	15 millilitres

Cups		
¼ cup (4 T)	56.8 millilitres	50 millilitres
⅓ cup (5⅓ T)	75.6 millilitres	75 millilitres
½ cup (8 T)	113.7 millilitres	125 millilitres
⅔ cup (10⅔ T)	151.2 millilitres	150 millilitres
¾ cup (12 T)	170.5 millilitres	175 millilitres
1 cup (16 T)	227.3 millilitres	250 millilitres
4½ cups	984.8 millilitres	1000 millilitres, 1 litre

Ounces — Weight		
1 oz.	28.3 grams	30 grams
2 oz.	56.7 grams	55 grams
3 oz.	85 grams	85 grams
4 oz.	113.4 grams	125 grams
5 oz.	141.7 grams	140 grams
6 oz.	170.1 grams	170 grams
7 oz.	198.4 grams	200 grams
8 oz.	226.8 grams	250 grams
16 oz.	453.6 grams	500 grams
32 oz.	917.2 grams	1000 grams, 1 kg

Pans, Casseroles

8 × 8-inch, 20 × 20 cm, 2L	8 × 2-inch round, 20 × 5 cm, 2L
9 × 9-inch, 22 × 22 cm, 2.5L	9 × 2-inch round, 22 × 5 cm, 2.5L
9 × 13-inch, 22 × 33 cm, 4L	10 × 4½-inch tube, 25 × 11 cm, 5L
10 × 15-inch, 25 × 38 cm, 1.2L	8 × 4 × 3-inch loaf, 20 × 10 × 7 cm, 1.5L
14 × 17-inch, 35 × 43 cm, 1.5L	9 × 5 × 3-inch loaf, 23 × 12 × 7 cm, 2L

Oven Temperatures

Fahrenheit	Celsius	Fahrenheit	Celsius	Fahrenheit	Celsius
175°	80°	300°	150°	425°	220°
200°	100°	325°	160°	450°	230°
225°	110°	350°	180°	475°	240°
250°	120°	375°	190°	500°	260°
275°	140°	400°	200°		

INDEX

Company's Coming — Taste The Tradition

SAVE $5.00

Mail to:
COMPANY'S COMING PUBLISHING LIMITED
BOX 8037, STATION "F"
EDMONTON, ALBERTA, CANADA T6H 4N9

Please send the following number of **Company's Coming Cookbooks** to the address on the reverse side of this coupon:

Qty.	Title	Each	Total
	150 DELICIOUS SQUARES	$9.95	
	CASSEROLES	$9.95	
	MUFFINS & MORE	$9.95	
	SALADS	$9.95	
	APPETIZERS	$9.95	
	DESSERTS	$9.95	
	SOUPS & SANDWICHES	$9.95	
	HOLIDAY ENTERTAINING	$9.95	
	COOKIES	$9.95	
	VEGETABLES	$9.95	
	MAIN COURSES	$9.95	
	PASTA	$9.95	
	CAKES (September 1990)	$9.95	
	JEAN PARÉ'S FAVORITES **VOLUME ONE** 232 pages, hard cover	$17.95	
Total Qty.	Total Cost of Cookbooks	$	
	Plus $1.00 postage and handling per copy	$	
Less $5.00 for every third copy per order		— $	
Plus International Shipping Expenses (add $4.00 if outside Canada and U.S.A.)		$	
Total Amount Enclosed		$	

Special Mail Offer: Order any 2 **Company's Coming Cookbooks** by mail at regular prices and **save $5.00** on every third copy per order.
Not valid in combination with any other offer.

Orders Outside Canada — amount enclosed must be paid in U.S. Funds.

Make cheque or money order payable to: "Company's Coming Publishing Limited

Prices subject to change after December 31, 1992.

Sorry, no C.O.D.'s.

Company's Coming — Taste The Tradition

SAVE $5.00

Mail to:
COMPANY'S COMING PUBLISHING LIMITED
BOX 8037, STATION "F"
EDMONTON, ALBERTA, CANADA T6H 4N9

Please send the following number of **Company's Coming Cookbooks** to the address on the reverse side of this coupon:

Qty.	Title	Each	Total
	150 DELICIOUS SQUARES	$9.95	
	CASSEROLES	$9.95	
	MUFFINS & MORE	$9.95	
	SALADS	$9.95	
	APPETIZERS	$9.95	
	DESSERTS	$9.95	
	SOUPS & SANDWICHES	$9.95	
	HOLIDAY ENTERTAINING	$9.95	
	COOKIES	$9.95	
	VEGETABLES	$9.95	
	MAIN COURSES	$9.95	
	PASTA	$9.95	
	CAKES (September 1990)	$9.95	
	JEAN PARÉ'S FAVORITES **VOLUME ONE** 232 pages, hard cover	$17.95	
Total Qty.	Total Cost of Cookbooks	$	
	Plus $1.00 postage and handling per copy	$	
Less $5.00 for every third copy per order		— $	
Plus International Shipping Expenses (add $4.00 if outside Canada and U.S.A.)		$	
Total Amount Enclosed		$	

Special Mail Offer: Order any 2 **Company's Coming Cookbooks** by mail at regular prices and **save $5.00** on every third copy per order.
Not valid in combination with any other offer.

Orders Outside Canada — amount enclosed must be paid in U.S. Funds.

Make cheque or money order payable to: "Company's Coming Publishing Limited

Prices subject to change after December 31, 1992.

Sorry, no C.O.D.'s.

GIVE *Company's Coming* TO A FRIEND!

Please send Company's Coming Cookbooks listed on the reverse side of this coupon to:

NAME _____

STREET _____

CITY _____

PROVINCE/STATE _____ POSTAL CODE/ZIP _____

GIFT GIVING — WE MAKE IT EASY!

We will send Company's Coming cookbooks directly to the recipients of your choice — the perfect gift for birthdays, showers, Mother's Day, Father's Day, graduation or any occasion!

Please specify the number of copies of each title on the reverse side of this coupon and provide us with the name and address for each gift order. Enclose a personal note or card and we will include it with your order . . .

. . . and don't forget to take advantage of the **$5.00 saving** — buy 2 copies of **Company's Coming Cookbooks** by mail and **save $5.00** on every third copy per order.

Company's Coming — We Make It Easy — You Make it Delicious!

GIVE *Company's Coming* TO A FRIEND!

Please send Company's Coming Cookbooks listed on the reverse side of this coupon to:

NAME _____

STREET _____

CITY _____

PROVINCE/STATE _____ POSTAL CODE/ZIP _____

GIFT GIVING — WE MAKE IT EASY!

We will send Company's Coming cookbooks directly to the recipients of your choice — the perfect gift for birthdays, showers, Mother's Day, Father's Day, graduation or any occasion!

Please specify the number of copies of each title on the reverse side of this coupon and provide us with the name and address for each gift order. Enclose a personal note or card and we will include it with your order . . .

. . . and don't forget to take advantage of the **$5.00 saving** — buy 2 copies of **Company's Coming Cookbooks** by mail and **save $5.00** on every third copy per order.

Company's Coming — We Make It Easy — You Make it Delicious!

Company's Coming — Taste The Tradition

SAVE $5.00

Mail to:
COMPANY'S COMING PUBLISHING LIMITED
BOX 8037, STATION "F"
EDMONTON, ALBERTA, CANADA T6H 4N9

Please send the following number of **Company's Coming Cookbooks** to the address on the reverse side of this coupon:

Qty.	Title	Each	Total
	150 DELICIOUS SQUARES	$9.95	
	CASSEROLES	$9.95	
	MUFFINS & MORE	$9.95	
	SALADS	$9.95	
	APPETIZERS	$9.95	
	DESSERTS	$9.95	
	SOUPS & SANDWICHES	$9.95	
	HOLIDAY ENTERTAINING	$9.95	
	COOKIES	$9.95	
	VEGETABLES	$9.95	
	MAIN COURSES	$9.95	
	PASTA	$9.95	
	CAKES (September 1990)	$9.95	
	JEAN PARÉ'S FAVORITES **VOLUME ONE** 232 pages, hard cover	$17.95	

Total Qty.			
	Total Cost of Cookbooks	$	
	Plus $1.00 postage and handling per copy	$	
Less $5.00 for every third copy per order		— $	
Plus International Shipping Expenses (add $4.00 if outside Canada and U.S.A.)		$	
Total Amount Enclosed		$	

Special Mail Offer: Order any 2 **Company's Coming Cookbooks** by mail at regular prices and **save $5.00** on every third copy per order. Not valid in combination with any other offer.

Orders Outside Canada — amount enclosed must be paid in U.S. Funds.

Make cheque or money order payable to: "Company's Coming Publishing Limited

Prices subject to change after December 31, 1992.

Sorry, no C.O.D.'s.

- -

Company's Coming — Taste The Tradition

SAVE $5.00

Mail to:
COMPANY'S COMING PUBLISHING LIMITED
BOX 8037, STATION "F"
EDMONTON, ALBERTA, CANADA T6H 4N9

Please send the following number of **Company's Coming Cookbooks** to the address on the reverse side of this coupon:

Qty.	Title	Each	Total
	150 DELICIOUS SQUARES	$9.95	
	CASSEROLES	$9.95	
	MUFFINS & MORE	$9.95	
	SALADS	$9.95	
	APPETIZERS	$9.95	
	DESSERTS	$9.95	
	SOUPS & SANDWICHES	$9.95	
	HOLIDAY ENTERTAINING	$9.9 5	
	COOKIES	$9.95	
	VEGETABLES	$9.95	
	MAIN COURSES	$9.95	
	PASTA	$9.95	
	CAKES (September 1990)	$9.95	
	JEAN PARÉ'S FAVORITES **VOLUME ONE** 232 pages, hard cover	$17.95	

Total Qty.			
	Total Cost of Cookbooks	$	
	Plus $1.00 postage and handling per copy	$	
Less $5.00 for every third copy per order		— $	
Plus International Shipping Expenses (add $4.00 if outside Canada and U.S.A.)		$	
Total Amount Enclosed		$	

Special Mail Offer: Order any 2 **Company's Coming Cookbooks** by mail at regular prices and **save $5.00** on every third copy per order. Not valid in combination with any other offer.

Orders Outside Canada — amount enclosed must be paid in U.S. Funds.

Make cheque or money order payable to: "Company's Coming Publishing Limited

Prices subject to change after December 31, 1992.

Sorry, no C.O.D.'s.

GIVE *Company's Coming* TO A FRIEND!

Please send Company's Coming Cookbooks listed on the reverse side of this coupon to:

NAME _____

STREET _____

CITY _____

PROVINCE/STATE _____ POSTAL CODE/ZIP _____

GIFT GIVING — WE MAKE IT EASY!

We will send Company's Coming cookbooks directly to the recipients of your choice — the perfect gift for birthdays, showers, Mother's Day, Father's Day, graduation or any occasion!

Please specify the number of copies of each title on the reverse side of this coupon and provide us with the name and address for each gift order. Enclose a personal note or card and we will include it with your order . . .

. . . and don't forget to take advantage of the **$5.00 saving** — buy 2 copies of **Company's Coming Cookbooks** by mail and **save $5.00** on every third copy per order.

Company's Coming — We Make It Easy — You Make it Delicious!

GIVE *Company's Coming* TO A FRIEND!

Please send Company's Coming Cookbooks listed on the reverse side of this coupon to:

NAME _____

STREET _____

CITY _____

PROVINCE/STATE _____ POSTAL CODE/ZIP _____

GIFT GIVING — WE MAKE IT EASY!

We will send Company's Coming cookbooks directly to the recipients of your choice — the perfect gift for birthdays, showers, Mother's Day, Father's Day, graduation or any occasion!

Please specify the number of copies of each title on the reverse side of this coupon and provide us with the name and address for each gift order. Enclose a personal note or card and we will include it with your order . . .

. . . and don't forget to take advantage of the **$5.00 saving** — buy 2 copies of **Company's Coming Cookbooks** by mail and **save $5.00** on every third copy per order.

Company's Coming — We Make It Easy — You Make it Delicious!